W9-BAR-369

Contents

101 COOL SCIENCE EXPERIMENTS

Cover Design: Hinkler Books Studio
Cover Illustration and Illustrations: Glen Singleton

 101 Cool Science Experiments
Published in 2005 by Hinkler Books Pty Ltd
17–23 Redwood Drive
Dingley VIC 3172 Australia
www.hinklerbooks.com

© Hinkler Books Pty Ltd 2004
This edition first published 2005
10 9 8 7 6 5 4 3
10 09 08 07 06

ISBN: 1 7415 7234 7
Printed and bound in China

101 COOL SCIENCE EXPERIMENTS

☆ **Introduction** ☆

 This book is full of simple science experiments to shock and amaze you. Ordinary materials like vinegar, string, eggs, and paper are used to make extraordinary things. They will help you find how science works, and why things happen the way they do. Most of all, these experiments are fun!

You will end up growing your own stalactites and be able to bounce an egg. Why not make a mobile out of gelatin, or dive a mini submarine into the depths of a bottle? Your kitchen will never be the same when you create your own underwater volcano.

Like to eat? Why not try baked ice cream? Yes, I do mean baked.

You will find most of the equipment you need for the experiments around the house. A good tip is to find an empty box and keep it stocked with things you might need. Don't throw out used jars, corks, or lengths of string. Why not store them in the box all ready for when you do your next experiment.

☆ **Acknowledgements** ☆

The experiments were tried, tested, and improved by the following very giggly children during their holidays and weekends – they had loads of fun. We hope you do too! ☆ Rebecca Chapman, ☆ Olivia Kenyon, ☆ Shivani Goldie, ☆ Katherine Jenkins and ☆ Verity Maton.

A special thanks to the following big people too! ☆ Dr. Greg Chapman, ☆ Dr. Kate Kenyon, ☆ Lois Goldthwaite, ☆ Dr. Paul Maton, and ☆ Ann Jenkins.

Helen Chapman

☆ ☆ **Experiment Rating**

Easy:	Medium:	Difficult:	Adult needed:

Wait and See

(1) The Bouncin' Egg

Rat's Rating

That's the first time I've ever seen an egg ride a pogo stick!

Anything's possible in Science I suppose!

Can an egg bounce without breaking?
Wait! Don't try it yet. Read what to do first.

You will need:
eggs, water, vinegar, flashlight, bowl ☆

Rat's Helpful Hint
Don't do this experiment in a hot bath. The eggs will cook and get hard-boiled. Also, don't try this at the end of the week - eggs hate Fry-days.

For this biology experiment –

1 Put 1 whole raw egg in a glass of water.

2 Put 1 whole raw egg in a glass of vinegar.

3 The eggs are the same aren't they? Now, leave them for a few hours.

4 Look at both eggs. Do they still look the same? The egg in the water is the same, but the egg in the vinegar has changed. The shell has begun to fizz. The acid in the vinegar dissolves the calcium carbonate that's in the shell.

5 Look carefully. Does the egg in vinegar still have its shell? Touch it. It now feels and looks like a rubber ball, doesn't it?

Hey! Go easy!

6

6 Leave both eggs alone for 7 days. After that time, take the egg in vinegar to a dark room and shine a flashlight at it. What do you see? The light bounces off the egg, doesn't it?

7 Take the egg out of the glass of vinegar. Hold the egg a little bit over a bowl.

8 Let the egg drop. Do you think it will splatter? Try it!

What Happens

Your egg bounces! Try it again getting a little higher each time. See how high you can make the egg bounce. What do you think will happen if you try to bounce the egg that was in the water? Hold it over the bowl and try.

No! NOT THE BOWL!!

Why

- A chemical change takes place in the egg when left in vinegar.
- The vinegar, which is an acid, reacts with the calcium carbonate of the eggshell.
- The change makes the shell go soft, then disappear. This is called "decalcification".
- The egg in the glass of water does not chemically change.

Fun Fact

You can make chicken bones so soft that you can bend them. Put a clean wishbone or leg bone into a jar of vinegar. Make sure the bones are completely covered. Leave them there for seven days. The bones will go so soft that you can twist them into a knot! Minerals in the bone make it strong and rigid. The vinegar takes away these minerals and the bones dissolve like the eggshell.

Just look at those legs! She's been soaking them in VINEGAR... You can tell!

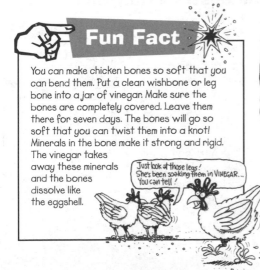

Mini Quiz
The word vinegar comes from two French words – "vin" which means wine and "aigre" which means sour. Vinegar has been in use for a long time, but how long?

Mini Answer ✓
It is known that vinegar was used in Babylon in 5,000 B.C.

② Grow a Stalactite

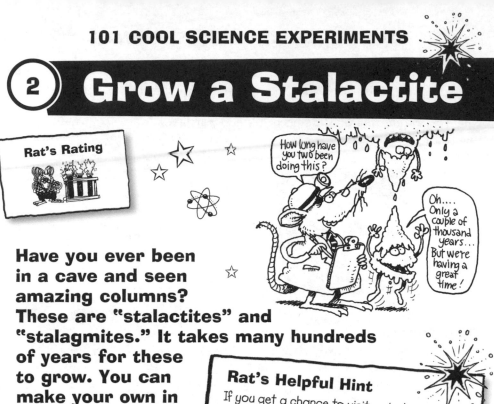

Rat's Rating

Have you ever been in a cave and seen amazing columns? These are "stalactites" and "stalagmites." It takes many hundreds of years for these to grow. You can make your own in just a few weeks!

Rat's Helpful Hint
If you get a chance to visit a dark cave, remember to hide around a corner. When someone passes by, leap out and shout "Boo!" Adults just love this!

You will need:
glass jars, baking soda or Epsom salts. (The salts take longer, but give you more shapes.) spoon, wool/cotton/string (any thread that will soak up water), paperclips, water, saucer

What to do for this chemistry experiment

1 Fill two clean jars with hot water.

2 Add as much baking soda to each jar as will dissolve.

3 Mix well so that the soda is dissolved completely.

4 Dip each end of the thread into the jars. The ends must be weighed down with paperclips, pencils, popsicle sticks, or nails to keep them in the jars.

5 Place a saucer between the jars to catch the drips.

6 Let the thread hang between the jars and over the saucer.

7 Leave the jars for 2 – 3 weeks. Will anything grow?

What Happens

A white stalactite grows down from the wool and a stalagmite grows up from the saucer.

Why

- The baking soda mix is carried up through the thread. This is called *capillary action*.
- The mix then drips onto the saucer.
- Over the days, the dripping water evaporates. It leaves a little of the baking soda behind.
- These bits of baking soda make a tiny stalactite and stalagmite.
- After months, these join. They make a single column like the one you see in a cave.

Fun Fact

One of the world's tallest stalagmites is in Slovakia. Cavers found the 106.9 feet (32.6 meters) tall stalagmite in 1964.

DANGEROUS!

WHAT'S THE VIEW LIKE FROM UP THERE?

Mini Quiz
What is the difference between stalactites and stalagmites?

Mini Answer ✓
Stalactites are the long rock columns that grow from the roof of a cave and hang down. Stalagmites look the same but they grow on the bottom of a cave and grow upward. When they meet, they make a column. They come from deposits of the mineral calcium carbonate in water that drips into the cave. To remember the difference between the two, think of this: stalactites hold tight ('tite') to the roof of the cave and stalagmites might (mite) reach the roof.

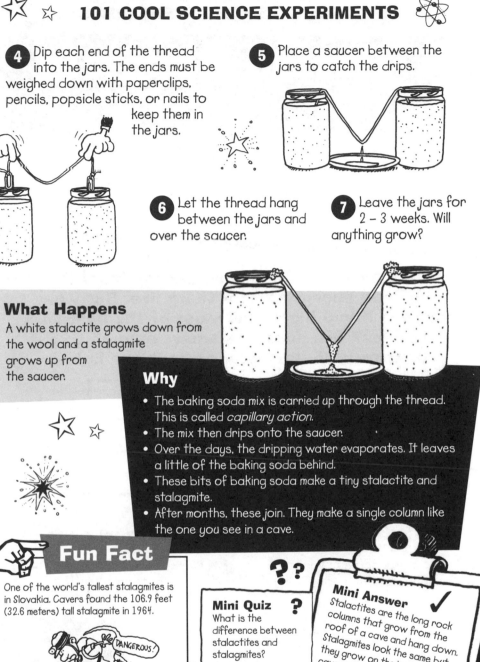

9

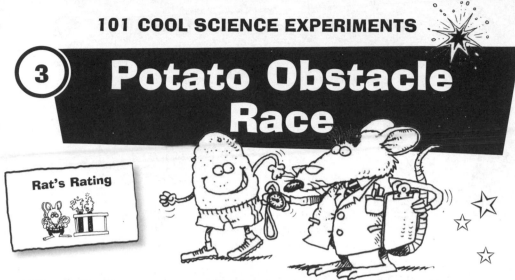

③ Potato Obstacle Race

Rat's Rating

Like all plants, potatoes turn energy from the sun into food energy to help them live. But what happens if you block out most of the light with obstacles? Are potatoes smart enough to get past your obstacles and reach the light?

You will need:
shoe box with lid, a sprouting potato – one with little white shoots growing out of it, scissors, potting soil, "obstacles" such as small boxes, thread spools, candy tubes, baby food jars, sunny days

What to do for this biology experiment

1 Cut a small coin size gap in the short side of the box

2 Put a handful of the potting soil in the corner of the shoebox. It must be at the opposite end from the hole you made.

3 Lay the potato on the soil.

Hmmm A nice and comfy piece of dirt

4 Put the "obstacles" in the box. The smaller the box, the less obstacles you will need.

5 Put the lid on. Place the box anywhere that gets lots of sun. Don't touch the box for 4 weeks.

6 When the 4 weeks are up, open the box. What do you see?

AHHRR MY EYES!

SHOES

What Happens

The shoot has made its way over, or around the obstacles you left in the way and has reached the hole.

1st

Why

- Plants have cells that are sensitive to light. The cells show the plant which way to grow.
- A tiny bit of light came into the shoebox. The potato shoot twisted until it reached the light.
- Plants will always grow towards the light. Even if they are buried deep in the soil.
- The shoot should be green, but it's white. This is because the *chlorophyll* that makes it green can't be made in the dark shoebox.

Fun Fact

In France, potato chips have been popular since the 1700s! It was the invention of the mechanical potato peeler in the 1920s that made potato chips go from a small specialty item to a top selling snack food.

If I could only invent the POTATO CHIP... I could be a wealthy man! I could even be a millionaire!! But I'd need to peel faster...

POTATO CHIPS

Mini Quiz
Why is it bad to eat potatoes that have turned green?

Mini Answer
Green potatoes are poisonous if you eat too many. The green is a chemical called *solanine*. This is made when the potatoes are left in sunlight. Even fluorescent lights at supermarkets can make potatoes turn green. Potato "eyes" also have lots of solanine, so don't eat them! When peeling potatoes, peel away all the green.

4 Cloudy Bacteria

Rat's Rating

Almost all our food has preservatives added. This is to stop food from going bad. But do preservatives really stop the growth of bacteria?

You will need:
salt, white vinegar, clear drinking glasses, chicken bouillon cube, measuring cup, measuring spoon, masking tape, marker

What to do for this zoology experiment

1 Dissolve 1 chicken bouillon cube in 1 cup of hot tap water.

2 Pour the mix into 3 glasses. Each glass must have the same amount.

3 Add 1 teaspoon of salt to a glass. Use the masking tape to label the glass "salt".

SALT

4 Add 1 teaspoon of vinegar to the 2nd glass. Label it "vinegar."

CONTROL

6 Place the 3 glasses in a warm place. Leave them for 2 days. Which glass is cloudier?

5 Label the 3rd glass "control", because it won't have a preservative.

VINEGAR

Boy! This is a warm spot!

And we've got 2 DAYS of it!

What Happens
The glass with the vinegar is clearer than the others. The "control" is the most cloudy.

CONTROL   SALT   VINEGAR

Why
- The cloudiness is made from large amounts of bacteria.
- The other two glasses have preservatives; therefore, are clearer than the control. This is because the preservatives slow the growth of bacteria.
- Vinegar stops the bacterial growth the best.
- Food preservatives are important to help stop food from going bad. They stop the growth of molds and bacteria.

Fun Fact
Cotton dishcloths and cellulose sponges are full of bacteria. These germs can make you sick. You can kill the bacteria. Just heat the cloths and sponges for 1 minute on high in your microwave oven.

There's no way I'm trying a hot sponge out of a microwave oven without sauce!

Mini Quiz
Are preservatives in food bad for you?

Mini Answer
For most people, preservatives are safe. Other people are very sensitive or even allergic to them. This is why packaged food with preservatives must have a clear label.

5 Fuzz Balls

I don't like the way that mold is staring at me!

Rat's Rating

Can mold be useful in making medicine? Does bacteria have an infectious laugh? Let's find out.

You will need:
oranges, lemons, or other citrus fruits, bowl, clear polythene bags (the type bread comes in), cotton balls

Rat's Helpful Hint
If you don't have time to do this experiment, just look behind the sofa, or under your bed. You're sure to find all sorts of moldy food.

What to do for this botany experiment

1 Place the fruit in a bowl. Leave it out in the air for 1 day.

2 Open the 2 bread bags. Put 1 orange, 1 lemon, and a wet cotton ball in each bag.

3 Tie the ends of the bags.

4 Place one bag in the refrigerator.

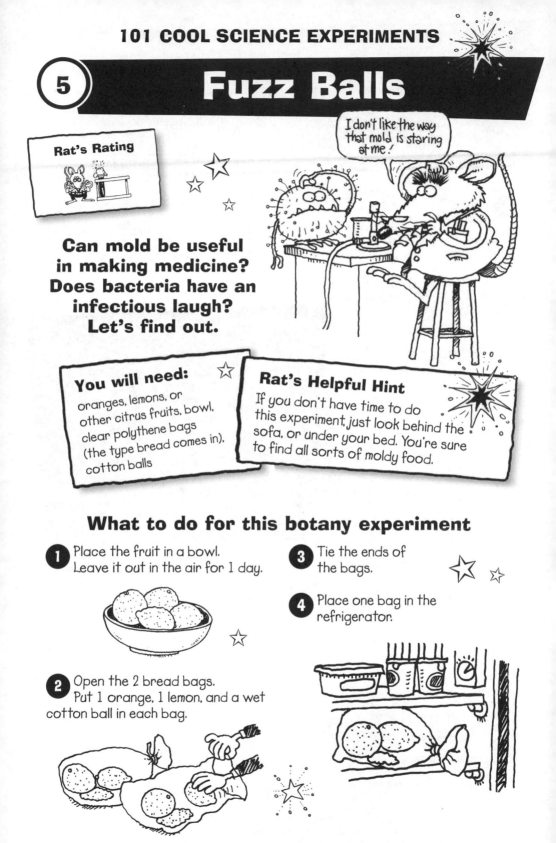

5 Place the other bag in a warm dark place.

6 Leave the bags closed for 2 weeks.

7 Check the fruit through the bags each day.

What Happens

The fruit in the refrigerator looks much the same. At worst, it may be a bit drier. The other fruit has turned into blue-green fuzz balls. This fuzzy growth on the outside of the fruit is *penicillin*.

EEEEE... That's some mighty ugly citrus fruit!

Why

- Mold is a form of fungus that makes tiny cells called *spores*.
- Spores are even tinier than dust particles! They float through the air.
- Mold grows faster in moist warm places. That is why foods become moldier in the summer.
- Keeping food cool slows the growth of mold. Freezing keeps foods fresh for even longer periods.
- Fungi are all around us. They usually don't reach the fruiting body stage. This is because there aren't enough nutrients and water available.

Fun Fact

Under a microscope, penicillin mold looks like a small brush. The Latin word for paintbrush is "penicillus". This is how penicillin got its name. The word pencil also comes from this Latin word, because brushes were used for writing.

Mini Quiz
How did an accident lead to the discovery that penicillin could kill bacteria?

Mini Answer ✔
Alexander Fleming discovered penicillin by accident. In 1928, he left an open dish of bacteria in his laboratory and after two weeks found mold growing on the bacteria. He saw that there was a clear zone where the bacteria had died. Fleming discovered that the mold had made a chemical that could kill bacteria and cure infections. Penicillin is still used today as an *antibiotic* to fight some infections.

You gotta see this! There's more than PENICILLIN living in your toothbrush! Where's it been?

In my MOUTH...

6 Rock and Dissolve

Rat's Rating

Love ya baby... Love you like a rock!

Can something as soft as rain dissolve something as strong as a rock?

You will need:
small drinking glasses, glass lemon juice, glass vinegar, glass water, 3 pieces white chalk

What to do for this chemistry experiment

1 Pour 1/2 glass lemon juice in glass 1. Pour 1/2 glass vinegar in glass 2. Pour 1/2 glass water in glass 3.

LEMON   VINEGAR   WATER

LEMON   VINEGAR   WATER

2 Put 1 piece of chalk in each of the glasses. Make sure part of the chalk is in the liquid.

3 Place the glasses where they won't be knocked over.

4 Check on the glasses over the next few days. What is happening?

What Happens

The chalk dissolves in the vinegar and in the lemon juice.

Why

- When you breathe out, you send carbon dioxide into the air.
- When carbon dioxide dissolves into raindrops, it makes rain become naturally acidic.
- Over time, this acid rain dissolves and erodes rocks.
- The chalk you used in the experiment is made of the rock limestone, or *calcium carbonate*.
- When acids react with limestone, they eat away at the rock and start to break it apart.
- Lemon juice and vinegar are acids. They're much stronger than acid rain, so erosion happens more quickly. You can see how acid rain can affect rocks over hundreds and thousands of years.

 **Fun Fact**

England's famous White Cliffs of Dover are made of great sheets of chalk, a form of calcium carbonate. If you lean against the cliffs, you get covered with white powder.

Stop rubbing yourself on the chalk cliffs and come play with your brother in the gravel... They'll use you at school to write on the blackboard!

Mini Quiz
What does the Great Pyramid of Giza have to do with chalk?

Mini Answer ✓
The Great Pyramid is mainly made from blocks of limestone. The fine white limestone came from a quarry on the other side of the Nile. Egyptians used copper chisels to cut their way down into the limestone. They slowly separated block after block from the rock face.

7

It's Not Easy Being Green

Rat's Rating

I think all you need is a little light my friend!

**"Leaf through" these green activities.
You'll find that looking green doesn't always
mean looking sickly.**

You will need:
pieces black paper,
indoor potted plant with
green leaves, scissors,
paper clip, tape

Rat's Helpful Hint
Make sure the plant you use is
alive. If you use a fake one, not
a lot will happen.

What to do for this botany experiment

1 Cut 2 pieces of black paper big enough to cover one leaf on the plant.

2 Sandwich the leaf between the two pieces of paper.

3 Clip the paper at the top and tape the sides.

4 Make sure that the leaf does not get any sunlight.

5 Wait for 7 days.

6 Uncover the leaf. Does it look different compared to the rest of the plant.

Why
- If plants don't get sunlight, they can't make chlorophyll.
- Chlorophyll is the chemical that gives leaves their green color.
- Without sunlight, the green pigment gets used up. It can't be replaced in the leaf. You end up with a leaf that loses its green color, and finally die.
- After a week without the covering, the leaf turns green again.

What Happens
The leaf is much paler than the other leaves on the plant. Now, watch the leaf over the next few days. See what happens to it when it gets sunlight again.

Fun Fact
Leaves are nature's food factories. Plants take water from the ground through their roots. They take a gas called *carbon dioxide* from the air. Plants use sunlight to turn water and carbon dioxide into glucose. Plants use glucose for energy and growing.

> I've just spent 7 days in some kind of scientific experiment...so I'm out to get some sun...some water...and plenty of nice fresh carbon dioxide

Mini Quiz ?
Do you find green plants living below 328 feet (100 meters) in the ocean?

Mini Answer ✓
No! Green plants only grow near the surface of the ocean. The deeper the water, the less plants are found. This is because green plants need sunlight. The sunlight totally disappears below 328 feet (100 meters) and the plants cannot live. Try something similar yourself. Put one plant in a sunny spot and another plant of the same variety in a dark cupboard and leave them for 7 days. The plant in the cupboard will be lighter in color and wilted.

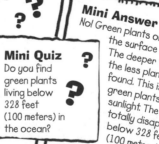

Fizzy, Flowing, and Funky

8 Super Starch

I may look like an uninteresting glob of corn starch...but I can do some amazing things!

Rat's Rating

Can something be a solid and a liquid at the same time? Sounds impossible! What do you think?

You will need:
cornstarch, measuring cup, mixing spoon, bowl

What to do for this chemistry experiment

1 Place 1 cup of cornstarch in a large bowl.

2 Add about 1/4 – 1/2 cup water and mix to a thick paste.

3 The powder is solid. The water is a liquid. Do you think the mixture will be a solid or a liquid?

4 Actually, it's both! With your hands, knead a handful of the mixture. It will become firm as long as you keep kneading.

5 Stop kneading. Quickly punch the mixture with your fist. It feels hard and may even crack.

7 Push your fingers into it very slowly. They will slide in as though the mixture is a liquid. Raise your hands and see it pour through your fingers.

6 Watch the mixture. Now that you have stopped kneading, it will return to its original form.

What Happens

As it stands, the mixture is a liquid – it's just water with powder floating in it. However, when you hit it, the water molecules are forced into the middle of each grain of powder, so the mixture is solid.

Why

- Some fluid mixtures have two forms.
- *Isotropy* is when a liquid becomes solid when moved.
- You can see this when walking on wet sand. The sand firms up below your feet when you first walk. It then becomes more liquid as your feet sink into it a moment later. If you run over the sand, it will feel hard. If you walk slowly, your feet will sink below the surface with each step.
- *Thixotropy* is the opposite of *isotropy*. *Thixotropy* is when the liquid mixture becomes more liquid as it is moved.
  - You might have done this when you hit the end of a ketchup bottle to get the ketchup to come out. The force temporarily makes the ketchup "runny," and it comes out easily from the bottle.

Fun Fact

Do you know that when you drink water you're drinking dinosaur spit? The water we have today is the same water that the dinosaurs drank. How can this be? Well, it can take a water molecule thousands of years to finish a cycle from ocean to sky to land and back to the ocean again. This is because the water may be trapped in ice for a very long time.

Does your water taste a little... Prehistoric?

Sure does! A little Jurassic actually!

Mini Quiz
What does starch have to do with newspapers?

Mini Answer ✓
Starch is used as a binder in the making of paper. It's the use of a starch coating that controls how much ink comes through when printing. Cheaper papers don't use as much starch. This is why your fingers get black when you hold newspaper.

(9) Looks Fishy to Me

Rat's Rating

FISHOMETER

You have heard of fish fingers, right? Well, did you know that fish have rings too? They don't wear them on their fingers because fish don't have fingers. But they do have them on their scales. The rings are special because they tell us something about the fish.

You will need:
scales from different types of fresh fish (using just one type is fine), small piece of dark paper, microscope, or magnifying glass

Rat's Helpful Hint
Remember that no mermaid likes to give away her age. So, no pinching scales from her tail ... especially when she's sitting on a rock singing.

What to do for this zoology experiment

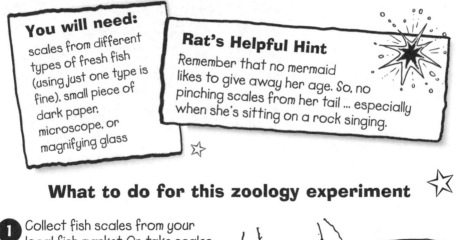

1 Collect fish scales from your local fish market. Or, take scales from a fish in your refrigerator. Leave your pet goldfish alone!

2 Place a dried scale on the dark paper.

3 Use a microscope to look at the ring pattern on the scale.

4 Count the wide, lighter rings. How many can you see?

5 Count the slim, darker rings. How many can you see?

6 What do you think the rings show us about the fish? Why are there are two types of rings?

What Happens

The number of rings on the scale is equal to the age of the fish. Are there some years the fish grew fast? Are there some years it grew slow? What environmental factors might explain this?

GROWTH RINGS! I've lost count!

Why

- As a fish grows larger, the scales grow larger too.
- Scales grow by adding rings around the outside edge of the scale. These rings look like the growth rings in the trunk of a tree.
- A scale may add anywhere from two to twenty rings a year.
- More rings mean more growth.
- Small reef fish usually live for only a few weeks or months. Other fish, such as the sturgeon can live to 50 years or more.

Fun Fact

Some Japanese restaurants serve raw puffer fish. Part of the fish is poisonous and the chef should take this away. However, each year over 20 people die after eating the wrong parts.

AHHR-SO Pufferfish full of hot air!

Mini Quiz What do fish scales and lipstick have in common?

Mini Answer ✔ Fish scales are used to make lipstick! Fish scales are shiny and silvery. They have a pearl essence. This essence is used in some lipsticks, nail polishes, and ceramic glazes. It makes them look glossy.

10 Invisible Ink

Rat's Rating

"PAINTING IN INVISIBLE INK" by I.C. LITTLE

You've heard of secret messages written in code, haven't you? But have you heard of secret messages being written with invisible ink?

You will need: ☆
lemon, saucer, water, teaspoon, toothpick, white paper, lamp

Rat's Helpful Hint
Why not send your invisible ink letter to a friend to read?

What to do for this chemistry experiment

1 Squeeze the lemon juice into the saucer.

2 Add a few drops of water and mix well with the spoon.

MIX MIX

3 Dip the toothpick into the lemon juice mix. Not too much or you'll make invisible blobs!

4 Use the toothpick to write a message on ordinary white paper. Thick paper works best.

5 When it dries, the writing will be invisible.

6 Heat the paper by holding it with the written side down near a light bulb. If an adult is helping, you can use heat from a stove or candle. What do you see?

What Happens
While it heats up, the invisible ink writing slowly becomes brown and visible. The words appear on the page.

This message is no longer a SECRET!

Why
- The juice of lemons has compounds of *carbon.*
- These compounds have almost no color when you dissolve them in water.
- When you heat them, the carbon compounds break down and turn black.

Fun Fact
Batteries have a chemical called an *electrolyte.* An electrolyte lets a chemical take place happen between the electrodes. The reaction makes electricity. In this experiment, lemon juice acts as an electrolyte.

My old lemons were flat in my flashlight... So I'm installing fresh ones

Mini Quiz
How does squeezing lemon juice onto fruit salad keep it fresh?

Mini Answer
When cut fruit like apples, pears, and bananas are left out in the air, they turn brown. This is because they react with the oxygen in the air. They become *oxidized.* Lemons have Vitamin C (ascorbic acid). Ascorbic acid slows the reaction between the chemicals in the fruit and the oxygen in the air. This keeps the color and taste of the other fruit.

11 Fizzy Rocket

Rat's Rating

Let us know if you make it to MARS!

What can fizzy tablets show us about the way rocket propellants release energy?

You will need:
antacid tablets of the same brand and type, jars, zip up plastic bag, watch or clock with second hand, rolling pin, water

What to do for this chemistry experiment

1 Half fill 2 jars with water that is the same temperature.

2 Put 1 antacid tablet into a zip up bag. Seal the bag.

3 Place the bag on a bench. Crush the tablet by pressing on it with the rolling pin.

4 Open the bag with the crushed tablet. Hold it over one of the jars.

5 Get your watch ready.

6 Pour the crushed tablet into a glass with water.

7 Time how long it takes the tablet powder to dissolve.

8 Pick up a whole tablet and drop it into the 2nd glass of water.

9 Time how long it takes the powder to dissolve completely.

Why
- By crushing the tablet into a powder, you've made its surface area bigger.
- The crushed tablet will now break up quickly in the water.
- The water immediately reacts with the powder.
- Rockets work in much the same way.
- The thrust of a rocket is higher when the burning surface of its fuel is higher.

What Happens
The crushed antacid tablet dissolves faster.

Fun Fact
You can do a similar, but much tastier test with small pieces of hard candy. Take two pieces of candy and crush one. Give the whole candy piece to a friend. You keep the crushed piece. Both of you then put the candy in your mouth, but don't chew it. Let the candy dissolve in your mouth. Whose candy will dissolve first?

MM-MM.... MM... M!
(READY)   (SET)   (SUCK!)

Mini Quiz
How does the space shuttle get off the ground?

Mini Answer ✓
Each U.S. Space Shuttle has two solid rocket boosters. These add additional thrust and acceleration to the main engines to help carry the shuttle into space. After two minutes, at an altitude of about 24 miles (38 km), the boosters separate and fall into the ocean where they are recovered and reused.

Floppy Disk

12

Rat's Rating

You know what a floppy disk is and you know what it does. But do you know what's inside it? Let's find out.

You will need:
3.5-inch floppy disk, butter knife, pencil, note paper

What to do for this computer science experiment

1 Ask an adult for a disk. (It might have important information on it.)

2 Look at the outside. What different parts can you find? Do any move?

3 Look for the places where the disk will come apart. Use the butter knife to pry open the metal rectangle. This is the shutter that folds over one edge of the disk. Pull it off. Put it to one side.

4 Put the knife in one of the slots. Gently pry apart the two flat halves of the disk. Don't snap the disk apart. If you do, you will lose the tiny spring that holds the shutter closed. Don't worry if the plastic at the corners of the disk breaks off or cracks.

5 Do the two halves of the disk look the same? What parts can you see? Write or draw a picture of where everything is before you go any further.

What Happens

When you take apart a 3.5-inch floppy disk, you'll end up with two plastic squares that hold the other, smaller parts. You should be able to see all the parts of the disk. These are: 1 metal shutter, 1 spring, 1 brown plastic circle with a metal center, 1 small black plastic rectangle with legs, 1 small plastic flap, 2 white paper rings, 2 plastic squares

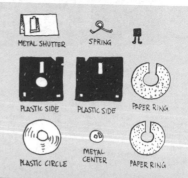

METAL SHUTTER   SPRING

PLASTIC SIDE   PLASTIC SIDE   PAPER RING

PLASTIC CIRCLE   METAL CENTER   PAPER RING

Why

- The metal *shutter* folds over one edge of the disk. That edge goes into the computer first. Inside the computer, the shutter slides over. The information on the disk is read through the rectangular slot.
- When the disk comes out of the machine, the *spring* snaps the shutter closed again. This stops dust or fingerprints from getting on the magnetic disk.
- The round piece of plastic is the *magnetic* disk. It is covered with iron oxide and can be magnetized. When you save information to a disk, a recording head makes a magnetic pattern on the iron oxide. The pattern stores your information. The computer can read this the next time you put in the disk.
- The *hub* is the metal center of the magnetic disk. The holes in the hub fit over spindles inside the computer. They hold the disk in place while it spins.
- The magnetic disk is between two white *paper rings*. These stay still while the disk spins. They clean the disk and take away tiny bits of dust.
- The little plastic rectangle is the *write-protect tab*. It moves to show a square gap. When the gap is open, the disk is locked. Your computer won't let you change anything.
- The *plastic flap* is hidden under a paper ring. A spring pushes the paper ring tight against the surface of the magnetic disk.

Fun Fact

A video is a bit like a floppy disk. A write-protect tab can be pulled out so no one can record over what you have on the tape. Videos also have a piece of paper or felt, and a spring that cleans the tape while it is moving.

Mom...you'll be proud of me! I've thoroughly cleaned your WEDDING VIDEO! It's now as clean as a whistle!

OUR WEDDING

Mini Quiz
Why is a floppy disk called floppy?

Mini Answer ✓
The nickname "floppy" came from the disk being flexible.

13 Let's Get Fizzy

Rat's Rating

You've all seen fire extinguishers. They work by taking away one part needed for a fire – oxygen. Try making your own extinguisher.

You will need:
candle, tall glass jar/drinking glass, short birthday cake candle, baking powder (not soda), matches, spoon, vinegar

What to do in this chemistry experiment
You will need an adult's supervision for this experiment.

1 Get an adult to light the candle.

2 Drip some wax in the bottom of your glass jar. Blow out the candle.

3 Stick the birthday cake candle in the wax so it stands upright. Keep the tip of the candle away from the rim of the jar. Your jar must be taller than the candle.

4 Put heaping spoonfuls of baking powder into the jar. Keep the powder away from the flame as much as possible.

5 Gently pour in some vinegar. There should be enough to make the powder fizzle and pop. What happens to the candle?

What Happens
After some time, the candle goes out.

Why
- Mixing the powder and the vinegar makes carbon dioxide gas.
- Unlike oxygen gas, the flame does not easily burn carbon dioxide.
- It is also heavier than the other gases that make up our atmosphere. The carbon dioxide sinks to the bottom of your jar.
- If enough gas is made, it will reach the level of the flame.
- When the candle can't keep burning its material with oxygen, it goes out.

Fun Fact
Mosquitoes don't just use their sight to find hosts to bite. They sense infra-red radiation coming from warm bodies and by chemical signals.

MY INFARED RADIATION HEAT SENSORS have failed me! I'll use my eyes from now on!

Mini Quiz
How do fire fighters put out fire using carbon dioxide?

Mini Answer ✓
Many fire extinguishers use compressed carbon dioxide to put out fires. By filling the space around the fire with the gas, the fire is suffocated. Unfortunately, since we need oxygen gas to live, breathing pure carbon dioxide also suffocates us.

(14) Eat Like a Dinosaur

Rat's Rating

Would you like a bucket full of rocks with your tree branches or whatever it is you eat?

Why would plant eating dinosaurs swallow stones? Try this experiment to find out.

You will need: ☆
2 rounded stones or pebbles, leaves, plastic bowl, scissors, teaspoon, water

Rat's Helpful Hint
Don't ever swallow stones or you'll end up as dead as the dinosaurs. ☆ ☆

What to do in this biology experiment.

1 Put 6 small leaves in the plastic bowl.

2 Use the scissors to cut up the leaves.

3 Add 1/4 teaspoon of water.

4 Hold the stones and grind the leaves between them.

I feel like a BRACHIOSAURUS eating lunch!

What Happens
The water turns green.

BURP

Why
- This is what happened in the dinosaur's stomach.
- A dinosaur swallowed stones called *gastroliths* to help it eat leaves.
- As the stones released the edible parts of the leaf, bacteria in the dinosaur's stomach rotted the food. This helped the dinosaur to digest its dinner.

Fun Fact
You can make your own fossil with modeling clay and a feather or a leaf. Roll the clay flat with a rolling pin. Press the feather or a leaf as hard as you can into the clay. Remove the feather. You will see the feather is preserved in the clay.

Now that will make A GREAT FOSSIL!

Mini Quiz
How can you feel dinosaur skin when dinosaurs are extinct?

Mini Answer ✓
All you do is touch your thumbnail with your finger. The hard stuff in your nail is called *keratin*. Dinosaur scales were made from exactly the same stuff.

15 Red Cabbage Rules

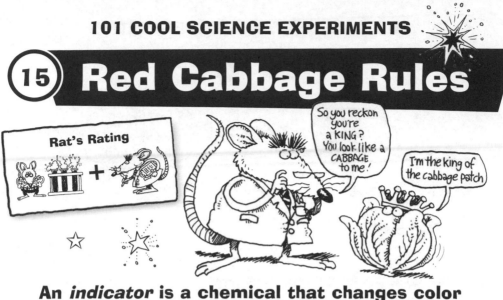

Rat's Rating

So you reckon you're a KING? You look like a CABBAGE to me!

I'm the king of the cabbage patch

An *indicator* is a chemical that changes color when an acid or alkali is added to it. Try making your own indicators and find out how to measure different substances.

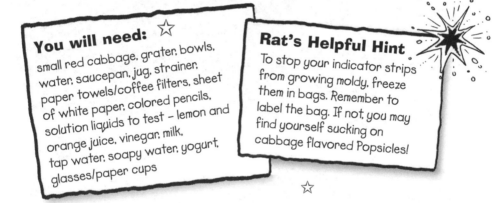

You will need:
small red cabbage, grater, bowls, water, saucepan, jug, strainer, paper towels/coffee filters, sheet of white paper, colored pencils, solution liquids to test – lemon and orange juice, vinegar, milk, tap water, soapy water, yogurt, glasses/paper cups

Rat's Helpful Hint
To stop your indicator strips from growing moldy, freeze them in bags. Remember to label the bag. If not, you may find yourself sucking on cabbage flavored Popsicles!

What to do in this chemistry experiment

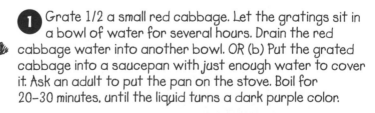

1 Grate 1/2 a small red cabbage. Let the gratings sit in a bowl of water for several hours. Drain the red cabbage water into another bowl. OR (b) Put the grated cabbage into a saucepan with just enough water to cover it. Ask an adult to put the pan on the stove. Boil for 20–30 minutes, until the liquid turns a dark purple color.

2 Let the cabbage juice cool and then strain it into a jug.

3 Cut 2 inch (5 cm) strips of paper towels.

4 Soak the strips of paper in the red cabbage juice until they turn bluish purple.

5 Lay the wet strips flat on a bench and leave them to dry. These are your indicator strips.

6 Put the liquids into separate paper cups.

7 Dip your paper indicator strips into the liquids.

LEMON   ORANGE   VINEGAR   MILK   TAP WATER   SOAPY WATER

8 Using pencils and the white paper, copy down the color that the paper strip turns.

9 Draw a picture, or write the name of the liquid that made the paper turn that color.

10 Use your notes to make a chart to show the different colors that different liquids turn the paper strips.

MY INDICATOR CHART

LEMON   ORANGE   VINEGAR   MILK

TAP WATER   SOAPY WATER   pH TESTER

What Happens

Your cabbage juice is a simple pH tester. It reacts differently to different substances. Once you know what color the juice turns in acids and alkalis, you can use it to test some other liquids.

Why

- Red cabbage has pigments that react differently to acids and alkalis.
- When you dip your strips into your substance and wait a few minutes, the color will fully develop.
- Your indicator strips will turn red-yellow in acid, green in neutral and purple blue in alkali.

Mini Quiz
What do all the colors mean on the pH scale?

Mini Answer ✓
Scientists invented the pH scale to tell you just how acidic a substance is. The scale goes from 1 which is very acidic through to 14 which is very alkaline. A pH of 7 is right in the middle of the scale and means a substance is neutral.

16 Blow Your Top

Rat's Rating

OOHH! That must have been a terrible headache!

Have you seen a real volcanoes erupt? Well, make your own. It's much safer.

You will need: ☆
flour, salt, cooking oil, water, large bowl, clean plastic soda bottle, baking pan, food coloring – red looks good – liquid detergent, baking soda, vinegar, water

Rat's Helpful Hint
This is a messy experiment. Make sure you know who's going to be cleaning up. Don't let your dog be the one to lick up the mess.

What to do in this chemistry experiment

1 Mix 6 cups of flour, 2 cups of salt, 4 tablespoons of cooking oil and 2 cups of water in a large bowl.

2 Using your hands, mix the ingredients until smooth and firm. Add more water to the mixture if needed.

3 Stand the soda bottle in the baking pan.

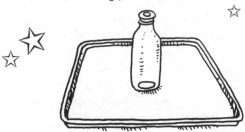

4 Mold the salt dough around the bottle. Make sure you don't cover up the bottle mouth or drop any dough in the bottle. You can build your volcano with as much detail as you like, or leave it plain.

5 Fill the bottle almost to the top with warm water.

6 Add drops of food coloring until you get a color you like.

7 Squeeze 6 drops of the liquid detergent into the bottle.

8 Add 2 tablespoons of baking soda.

9 Slowly pour vinegar into the bottle and jump back quickly. What do you think will happen?

What Happens

The "lava" flows out of your volcano.

VESUVIUS erupting NOW!

Why

- Mixing baking soda and vinegar makes a chemical reaction.
- A chemical reaction is where one substance is chemically changed to another.
- All chemical reactions are about the making or destroying of bonds between atoms in which carbon dioxide gas is made – the same gas that bubbles in a real volcano.
- The gas bubbles build up in the bottle. They force the liquid "lava" mixture up and over the mouth of your volcano.

Fun Fact

Over the long term, volcanic eruptions can help us. Volcanic materials break down and weather so that they form fertile soils.

Yep! This should be a great place for a farm... in about a MILLION YEARS

Mini Quiz
Where does the word "volcano" come from?

Mini Answer
The word 'volcano' comes from the island of Vulcano, near Sicily in Italy. A century ago, the local people believed that Vulcano was the chimney of the forge of Vulcan. Vulcan was the blacksmith of the Roman gods.

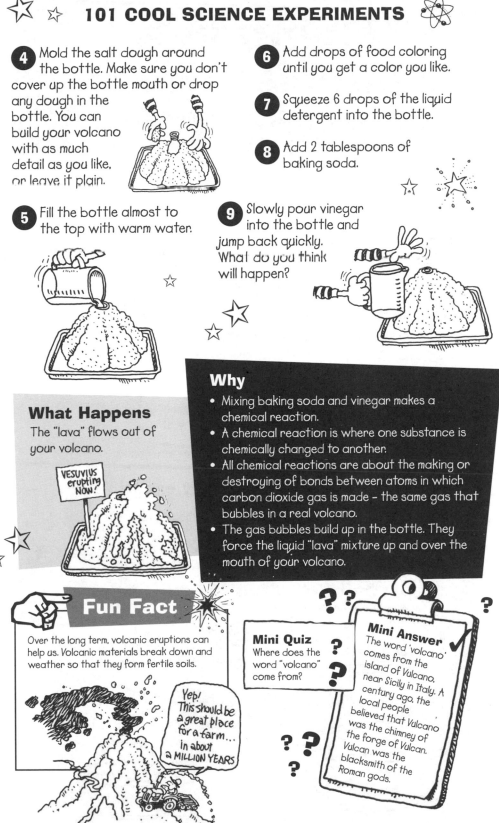

Living in a Material World

Rat's Rating

Could I interest you in one of my CRINKLE CUT CRISPS?

I DON'T MIND IF I DO!

Feeling energetic? It might be thanks to all those potatoes you've been eating! Let's see how.

> **You will need:**
> large potatoes, vegetable peeler, chopping board, grater, large clean handkerchief, small mixing bowl, water

What to do in this chemistry experiment

1 Ask an adult to help you peel and grate 3 large potatoes over a chopping board.

2 Half fill the bowl with water.

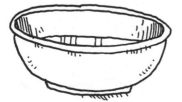

3 Put the grated potato into the handkerchief. Tie up the handkerchief.

4 Dip the handkerchief into the water. Squeeze it very hard into the bowl.

5 Keep dipping the handkerchief into the water and squeezing it out after each dipping. What is happening to the water? Is it very cloudy?

6 Leave the water in the bowl for 1 hour.

7 Can you see the white powder that has settled on the bottom of the bowl?

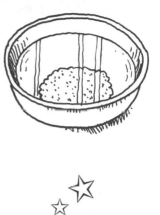

8 Carefully pour off as much of the clear water above the powder as you can. Leave the powder a couple of hours to dry out. What have you made?

Why
- Plants and animals make starch as a way of storing sugars.
- Potatoes, rice, barley, and wheat have large amounts of starch.
- When you eat foods high in starch, chemicals in your digestive juices change the starch to sugars that can be used by your body for quick energy.
- Starch is also put on cloth to give it weight and make it smooth. The starch you have made can be used this way when the cloth is ironed.

What Happens
The powder you have made is *starch*.

Fun Fact

A soda cracker is made of flour (which is a starch), water and baking powder. It has no sugar. If you chew a cracker and hold it in your mouth for 5 minutes, the taste of the cracker changes. There is a special chemical in your saliva that breaks the links in the starch chains so those sugar molecules are released.

I've had the other half of this soda cracker in my mouth for over a week now... and it's certainly changed...

INFACT.... IT'S TRYING TO CLIMB OUT!

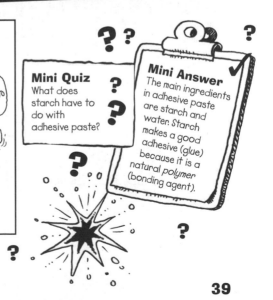

Mini Quiz
What does starch have to do with adhesive paste?

Mini Answer
The main ingredients in adhesive paste are starch and water. Starch makes a good adhesive (glue) because it is a natural polymer (bonding agent).

18 On Your Mark – Go!

Rat's Rating

If I were a GAMBLING RAT and not a LAB RAT. My money would be on this speedy looking black pen over here!

You've heard of horse racing and car racing, but did you know that marker pens could race each other?

You will need:
4 different brands of black markers, white coffee filter paper/ paper towels, clear drinking glass, pencil, clothespins

What to do in this biology experiment

1 Cut a rectangle out of the coffee filter. The width of the paper must fit easily in the glass. But the top of the filter paper must stick out!

2 Using a pencil, draw a line about 1 inch (2.5 cm) up from the bottom of the filter paper.

3 Using each black marker place a small dot along the line. Don't put the dots too close together.

4 Put the filter paper in the glass.

5 Clip the clothespins to the paper. Rest the clothespins across the top of the glass to stop the paper from slipping down.

6 Adjust the clothespins so the filter paper just touches the bottom of the glass.

7 Lift the filter paper out without unclipping the clothespins. Put it to one side.

8 Put a 1/4 inch (.05 cm) of water in the glass.

9 Put the glass in a place where it won't be bumped.

10 Slowly and carefully, lower the filter paper back into the glass. The clothespins will stop it from slipping down.

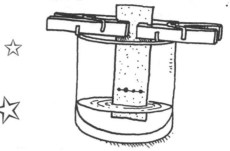

11 Don't touch the experiment, or it will go crazy!

12 Wait 5 minutes and see what has happened. Check again in another 5 minutes. Do you think the different black dots will do different things?

13 Once any changes have stopped, take the filter paper out of the glass or it will ruin the experiment.

What Happens

You will start to see different colors. Some of the markers might reach the top faster than others, or some might be more colorful. It all depends on what pens you use.

Why

- Most black markers are made from colored pigments or dyes, and water.
- The water in the ink carries the pigments up the filter paper.
- As the water dries, the pigments stay on the paper.
- The pigments dissolve when the filter is dipped in water.
- Some pigments move up the paper faster than others. They travel at different speeds. This depends on how large the pigment molecule is and how much the pigment is attracted to the paper.

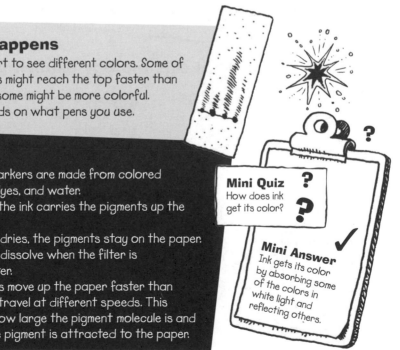

Mini Quiz ?
How does ink get its color? ?

Mini Answer ✓
Ink gets its color by absorbing some of the colors in white light and reflecting others.

19 Are You Absorbing This?

Rat's Rating

Wonder what's for lunch?

Did you manage to digest any of what I just said? You look totally absorbed in something else

Your intestines play a major role in absorbing the food you eat. Let's see how they work.

You will need:
masking tape, narrow glass jar, water, paper towels, marker

What to do in this biology experiment

1 Stick a piece of masking tape down the side of the jar.

2 Fill the jar with water. Mark the level on the tape with your marker.

3 Fold one sheet of paper towel in half four times to make a small square.

4 Dip the paper square into the jar of water. Make sure all the paper is under water.

5 Remove the wet paper. Mark the new water level on the tape.

6 Refill the jar with water to the same level as before.

7 Lay three sheets of paper towels on top of each other.

8 Fold them in half four times to make a small square.

9 Dip the paper square into the water.

10 Remove the wet paper. Mark the water level.

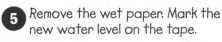

What Happens

The three sheets of folded paper towels removed much more water than the one sheet.

Why

• Folding the three sheets of paper made them smaller. But it did not change the way they soaked up water.
• The folded sheets act like the tissue inside the intestines of animals. Both are able to absorb large quantities of liquid. This is because of the makeup of their cells and their available surface area.

Fun Fact

Some materials absorb water better than others. Use a rubber band to tie different types of material (cotton, wool, cheesecloth, leather, fleece) to the top of clean empty jars. Carefully drip one teaspoon of water onto each jar. Do this a few times. Take away the material. See which jars have the most water. These materials will be less absorbent. The jars with very little water inside have absorbent material.

Who's the anti-social jar down the end with the lid on?

Mini Quiz
Your intestine has a large absorbing surface. How long is it?

Mini Answer ✓
Your intestine reaches from the lower end of your stomach to your bottom. This narrow tube coils around the abdominal cavity for about 28 feet (8.5 m). Its inner walls are lined with many folds of soft absorbing tissue.

20 Wax Factor

Rat's Rating

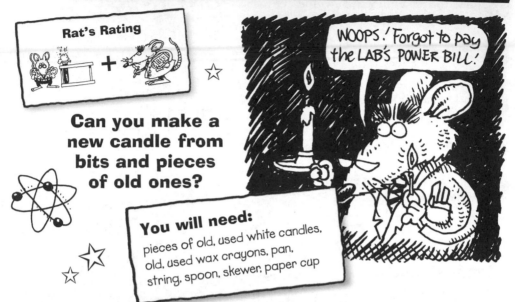

WOOPS! Forgot to pay the LAB'S POWER BILL!

Can you make a new candle from bits and pieces of old ones?

You will need:
pieces of old, used white candles, old, used wax crayons, pan, string, spoon, skewer, paper cup

What to do in this chemistry experiment

1 Put the candles and the wax crayons in a pan.

2 Ask an adult to melt them slowly over a low heat. Stir gently to swirl the mix together.

3 While the wax is melting, make a small hole in the bottom of a paper cup with a skewer.

4 Thread the string through.

5 Tie a knot underneath. The string should be long enough so you can hang your candle to dry.

6 Ask an adult to pour the wax into the paper cup.

7 Hang it up by its long string to dry. What happens?

What Happens

The wax will turn hard. To use your new candle, snip the string at the top and the bottom. Leave just enough at the top to use for the wick. It is very IMPORTANT to remove the paper cup before you light your new candle.

Why

- Wax can change from a solid to a liquid when it is heated.
- It will become a solid again when it cools.

SNIP

Fun Fact

On Earth, gravity-driven buoyant convection makes a candle flame a teardrop-shape. This means that the air in the flame expands and becomes lighter. The lighter air rises up. This is the convection current. In microgravity, there are no convective flows. The candle flame is round because the vaporized wax spreads out from the wick and the oxygen goes into the flame from surrounding air.

Do you mind if I blow out the candles now before they burn out... And we discuss the finer points of GRAVITY DRIVEN BUOYANT CONVECTION a little later!

Mini Quiz
Where do candles come from?

Mini Answer
Candles came from the Romans. Ancient Egyptians used tallow-soaked torches, but the Romans had candles with a wick. These were used to help people travel through dark nights, lighting homes, and places of worship.

(21) Streaky Paper

Rat's Rating

Want to wrap a small gift but don't have any wrapping paper. Try making your own by using ordinary sheets of white paper. Here's how.

GGRRRRR

You will need:
color chalk – go for colors that will look good together, white paper – amount depends on how much swirly paper you want to make, paper or plastic cups, rolling pin, vinegar, zip lock plastic bags, plastic spoon, large plastic bowl, newspaper, water, cooking oil

What to do in this chemistry experiment

1 Place sheets of newspaper on a table.

2 Fill the bowl with water.

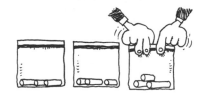

3 Add 2 tablespoons of vinegar.

4 Place the bowl in the center of the newspaper.

5 Place small pieces of different colored chalk into separate zip lock up bag. Zip up the bag.

6 Use the rolling pin to crush the chalk into a fine powder.

7 Tip each powered chalk color into its own cup.

8 Pour 1 tablespoon of oil into each cup. Stir well with the plastic spoon.

9 Pour the contents of each cup into the bowl of water. The chalky colored oil should form large colored pools on top of the water.

10 Carefully lay each piece of of white paper on the surface the water.

11 Lift out and place on the sheets of newspaper to dry. This will take about 24 hours.

12 When the papers are fully dried, carefully wipe off any surface chalk grains with a paper towel. What do you have left?

What Happens
The colored oil sticks to the paper and makes swirls and streaky patterns.

Why
- Negative and positive charged molecules are attracted to each other.
- The molecules of chalk (calcium carbonate) and vinegar (acetic acid) and water and the surface of the paper all chemically mix to make a chemical bond.
- This causes the streaky colors to stick to the paper.

Fun Fact
A film of oil on water will kill mosquito larvae. This is because the oil clogs up the snorkel that the larvae use to breathe.

WOH! TAKE A DEEP BREATH GUYS! Someone up there is making that STREAKY PAPER BIRTHDAY WRAP.!!

Mini Quiz Where was the world's worst oil spill?

Mini Answer The world's worst oil spill to date was in the Gulf of Mexico in 1979. The well blew out on June 3 and poured 900,000 barrels of oil into the Gulf after just one month. It made a 40,000 sq. miles (103,600 sq. km) oil slick. The spill lasted for 9 months.

(22) Gelatin Mobile

You're going to have to stop being so nervous and stop wobbling like jelly... you'll ruin the photo!

Rat's Rating

Gelatin is used to make pill capsules, heart valves, photographic film, and of course fruit-flavored desserts. But can you make a mobile with it?

You will need:
plain gelatin, water, food color, plastic lid with rim, saucepan, egg slice, paper towels, cookie cutters, drinking straw, scissors, cooling rack

Rat's Helpful Hint
Why not color your mobile to match a festivity such as Orange for Halloween, Red for Valentine's Day or Green for St. Patrick's Day?

What to do in this chemistry experiment

1 Put 5 Tablespoons (75 ml) of water and 3-5 drops of food coloring in the saucepan.

2 Ask an adult to put the saucepan over a low heat.

3 Tip in the 3 envelopes of unflavored gelatin and stir until it dissolves.

4 Cook and stir for 30 seconds or until the mixture is thick.

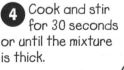

5 Pour the mixture into a plastic lid with a rim.

6 Push the air bubbles out with a spoon.

7 Let the gelatin cool for 45 minutes.

8 Use an egg slice to carefully lift the gelatin from the lid. What have you made?

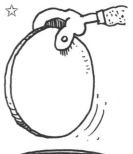

What Happens

You have made an elastic gel. Use the cookie cutters to make different shapes. Scissors are great for making spirals. Make holes in the gel with a plastic drinking straw so you can hang your shapes. Dry your shapes on a cooling rack, or hang them on string to dry. The gelatin will be hard like plastic in 2-3 days.

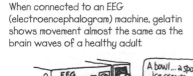

Why

- Gelatin is actually a protein called *collagen*.
- Collagen molecules line up to make fibers. These fibers don't dissolve in water.
- The fibers form a network that hold cells in place.
- When collagen is heated it breaks down to make a simpler protein called gelatin.
- Gelatin does dissolve in water. When a gelatin solution cools, it makes a semi solid mass or gel.
- A network of gelatin molecules trap the water in gelatin. It does this in much the same way as collagen molecules trap water.

Fun Fact

When connected to an EEG (electroencephalogram) machine, gelatin shows movement almost the same as the brain waves of a healthy adult.

A bowl... a spoon ...ice cream and custard!

I'm picking up excessive brain waves! ... What are you worrying about?

Mini Quiz
Where does gelatin come from?

Mini Answer
Gelatin is extracted by boiling in water (or acid) the bones, tissue, hooves, and ligaments of slaughtered meat-producing animals.

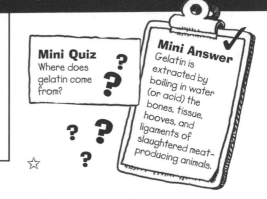

23 Save Our Silver

Rat's Rating

NOW....NOW!
We don't use
silver relics
for
Scientific
Experiments!

Silver is a bright and shiny metal. But it becomes stained when it reacts with sulfur in the air. Can you save the silver from being stained forever?

You will need:
dirty piece of silver, big bowl, aluminum foil, water, electric jug/microwave oven, kitchen mitts, baking soda

What to do

1 Line the bottom of the bowl with the aluminum foil.

2 Place your piece of silver on top of the foil. Make sure the silver touches the foil.

3 Ask an adult to heat the water to boiling.

4 Remove the water from the heat and place it in a sink.

5 Add about 1/2 cup of baking soda for each 1/2 gallon (1.2 litre) of water. The mixture will froth a bit and may spill over. This is why you put it in the sink!

6 Pour the hot baking soda and water mixture into the bowl. Make sure the silver is completely covered. Can you see any change in the silver?

Why

- When silver stains, it mixes with sulfur and makes *silver sulfide.*
- Silver sulfide is black. When a thin coating of silver sulfide forms on the surface of silver, it makes the silver all dark.
- You used a chemical reaction to change the silver sulfide back into silver.
- The silver sulfide reacted with the aluminum foil. In the reaction, sulfur atoms moved from silver to aluminum. This frees the silver metal and makes aluminum sulfide.
- The reaction between silver sulfide and aluminum takes place when both are in the baking soda. The reaction is faster when the solution is warm. The baking powder mix carries the sulfur from the silver to the aluminum. The aluminum sulfide sticks to the aluminum foil.
- The silver and aluminum must be in contact with each other. This is because a small electric current flows between them during the reaction. This is called an *electrochemical reaction.* Reactions like this are used in batteries to make electricity.

What Happens

The stain begins to disappear. If the silver is only lightly stained, all of the stain will disappear within several minutes. If the silver is badly stained, you may need to reheat the baking soda and water mixture, and give the silver several treatments to remove all of the stain.

BEFORE   AFTER

Fun Fact

Did you know that bacteria in our mouths feed on left over food particles and make smelly sulfur compounds? These sulfur compounds give breath its bad smell.

I just had the most yummy bit of cherry pie !

Well, remember that T-Bone steak last Tuesday? It's doing quite nicely over here.

Mini Quiz
Why is silver so shiny? ❓

Mini Answer
Silver is shiny because it is a very reflective metal. This means it can be polished to "give back" as much light as hits it.

Twister

24

Rat's Rating

WHOA! What have I created? A TWISTER? Oh... It's only a Mobius strip!

Can there ever be a place where inside and outside is one and the same?

You will need:
sheet of paper, scissors, pen, masking tape

What to do in this topology experiment

1 Cut the paper into a long rectangle about 1 inch (2 cm) wide.

2 Hold the strip out straight.

3 Give it a half twist (180 degrees). Use the masking tape to stick the two ends together.

4 Hold the edge of the strip against the tip of a pen.

5 Draw a line down the center of the strip. Don't take the pen off the paper.

6 Turn the paper and keep on drawing the line. You will move the paper as you go along. Do not stop until your line meets up with your starting point.

7 Take off the masking tape. Look at the paper. What have you done?

What Happens

You have drawn on both sides of the paper without lifting your pen! Now, tape it back how it was before (with a half twist). With the scissors cut the strip along the center line that you drew. Can you guess what you will make? You have made a chain that is twice as long as your original loop!

Why

- Your shape is known as a *Mobius* strip.
- When you twisted your strip, the inside and outside became one continuous surface.
- When you cut the strip, it became one longer chain. But it still had only one continuous surface.
- Now, try the experiment again. This time give the paper a full twist. You'll be surprised at what you see.

Fun Fact

During the early 1800s, the German mathematician August Mobius helped develop a study in geometry that is known as *topology*. Topology explores the properties of a geometrical figure that do not change when the figure is bent, or stretched.

I don't know what I'm making. I was going to call it a MOBIUS STRIP... But I think I'll just call it .... a mess!

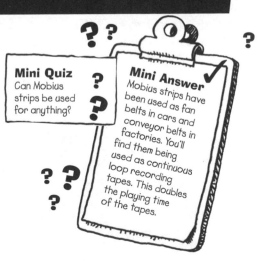

Mini Quiz
Can Mobius strips be used for anything?

Mini Answer
Mobius strips have been used as fan belts in cars and conveyor belts in factories. You'll find them being used as continuous loop recording tapes. This doubles the playing time of the tapes.

(25) Fantastic Plastic

Rat's Rating

A bottle of milk and a plastic bag ...all in one!

Plastic can be natural when it's made from something like oil or synthetic when made from material like nylon. But can plastic come from something as natural as milk?

You will need:
full cream milk, measuring cup, small saucepan, small jar, vinegar, tea strainer

What to do in this chemistry experiment

1 Pour 1/2 cup milk (125 mls) into a small saucepan.

2 Ask an adult to heat the milk until it simmers.

3 When the milk curdles and goes lumpy, stir in 3 teaspoons of vinegar.

4 Keep adding more vinegar until the mixture starts to gel.

5 Ask an adult to take the saucepan off the heat.

6 Pour off the liquid through a tea strainer.

7 Tip the lumps of curd into a jar.

8 Wait about 1 hour for the lumps to cool.

9 Slowly pour off any more water. What do you have left?

What Happens

You've made plastic! Why not dress up like Miss Muffet? You can sit outside with your plastic curds and see if a plastic spider comes along to eat them!

I might be a plastic spider... But that doesn't mean I have to like eating PLASTIC?

Why

- The plastic forms because of a chemical reaction.
- This reaction is between the *casein* in the milk and the *acetic acid* in the vinegar.
- When the milk and acid interacts, the milk separates.
- It separates into a liquid and a solid made of fat, minerals, and protein casein. This is made up of very long molecules that bend like rubber until they become hard. The same thing happens when milk curdles.

Fun Fact

Plastic bags and other plastic garbage thrown into the ocean kill as many as 1,000,000 sea creatures every year!

Mini Quiz
It takes five years for a milk carton to break down and return to the earth. How long does take a plastic bag?

Mini Answer ✓
It takes 400 years for a plastic sandwich bag to break down and return to the earth.

All Fall Down

(26) The Suspenseful Egg

Can you imagine something that doesn't float or sink when put in a liquid?

You will need:

large glass jar, egg, water, teaspoon, salt

What to do in this forces experiment

1 Half fill a glass jar with freshwater. Put a raw egg into the jar. It sinks, doesn't it?

2 Take out the egg.

3 Add 2 teaspoons of salt to the water. Mix well.

4 Take the same egg and put it in the jar. Watch the egg. What happens?

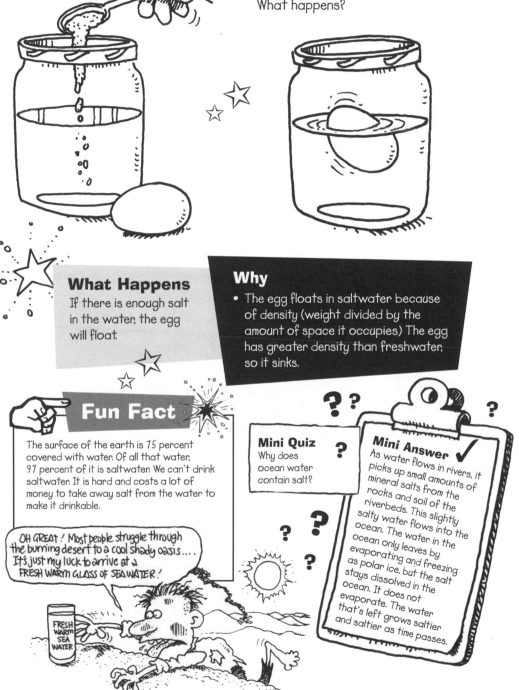

What Happens

If there is enough salt in the water, the egg will float.

Why

- The egg floats in saltwater because of density (weight divided by the amount of space it occupies) The egg has greater density than freshwater, so it sinks.

Fun Fact

The surface of the earth is 75 percent covered with water. Of all that water, 97 percent of it is saltwater. We can't drink saltwater. It is hard and costs a lot of money to take away salt from the water to make it drinkable.

OH GREAT! Most people struggle through the burning desert to a cool shady oasis.... It's just my luck to arrive at a FRESH WARM GLASS OF SEA WATER!

FRESH WARM SEA WATER

Mini Quiz

Why does ocean water contain salt?

Mini Answer ✔

As water flows in rivers, it picks up small amounts of mineral salts from the rocks and soil of the riverbeds. This slightly salty water flows into the ocean. The water in the ocean only leaves by evaporating and freezing as polar ice, but the salt stays dissolved in the ocean. It does not evaporate. The water that's left grows saltier and saltier as time passes.

Loop the Loop

(27)

Rat's Rating

So what are your thoughts on becoming the first toy dog in orbit..?

Ever wondered how satellites stay in orbit? Or why laundry in a washing machine is pushed against the sides during the spin cycle? Two forces, that of *gravity* and *centrifugal* force is the reason. Try these experiments to see how these forces work.

You will need:
rope 24 inches (60 cm) long, bucket, soft rubber ball ☆

Rat's Helpful Hint
Test forces at a fair or theme park. Go on one of those rides where you stand up while spinning around and the floor drops out from underneath you. It's another fun way to test forces.

What to do in your forces experiment

1 Tie the rope tightly to the handle of the bucket.

2 Put the ball in the bucket.

3 Go outside where there is no risk of you hitting anything.

4 Hold the bucket by the rope.

5 Whirl the bucket in the air as fast as you can.

What Happens

If you haven't hit anything, or anyone, the ball will stay in the bucket even when it turns upside down. For a satellite, it's the gravity of earth, and not a string that stops it flying out of orbit.

Why

- Centrifugal force – the force made by the whirling action – equals the force of gravity.
- This keeps the ball from falling out of the bucket.
- It pulls the ball against the sides of the bucket rather than down and out of it.
- Centrifugal force is directed away from the center by the rotating bucket. It is a "fleeing from the center" force.

Fun Fact

Want to feel the force of energy? Stretch a rubber band out suddenly. Then place it against your cheek. Feel the warmth? That is the stored energy trying to escape as heat!

What are you trying to do with that rubber band? Show energy escaping as heat?

NO... IT'S OUT OF CONTROL... WE'RE HEADING FOR A MELTDOWN!!

Mini Quiz

What is the difference between *Centripetal* force and *Centrifugal* force?

Mini Answer

Tie a ball to a long piece of string. Spin it around over your head. Centripetal force tries to pull the ball inward towards the center of the spin. Centrifugal force tries to throw the ball off in a straight line.

28 # Candles Rock

The center of gravity is that point in an object where there is as much weight on one side as the other.

You will need:
blunt knife or scissors, long candle, long nail, drinking glasses, saucers

What to do in this forces experiment

1 Scrape away some wax from the flat end of the candle so you can see the wick.

2 Push a long nail through the exact middle of the candle.

3 Rest the nail over both glasses.

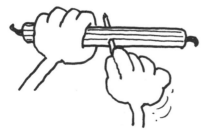

4 Put the saucers under each end of the candle.

5 Now you have a seesaw, but can you make it rock?

6 Ask an adult to light the wicks at both ends. Watch and see what happens.

What Happens

The candle rocks up and down.

Why

- A drop of hot wax falls from one end of the candle. This end rises because it is a bit lighter. Moments later, a drop falls from the other end of the candle and so it goes on.
- The balance of the candle is always being upset. This results in the candle continuing to rock up and down.

Fun Fact

If you lay a potted plant on its side and leave it for a week, something amazing happens. The plant's stem will turn upwards! Plants have a chemical called auxin. This makes plant cells grow long. Gravity pulls the auxin down. This builds up along the bottom of the stem. The cells grow longer where the auxin build up makes the stem turn upward.

OK! Obviously a plant with more than its fair share of AUXIN!

Mini Quiz

Do men and women have a different center of gravity?

Mini Answer ✓

Yes, they do! Most women have their center of gravity in the hip area. Men have it in their upper body. Try it yourself. Stand with your toes touching a wall. Place one foot behind the other. Take three steps back from the wall. Have someone place a stool between you and the wall. Lean over and place the top of your head against the wall. Your legs should be at about a 45-degree angle with your body.

Holding the edge of the stool, pick it up and hold the seat against your chest. Keeping the stool against your chest, try to stand up. If you have a low center of gravity (female), the weight of the stool will not stop you standing up. If you have a high center of gravity (male), the weight of the stool makes you so top heavy that you can't stand up.

(29) Are You a Swing King?

Rat's Rating

How does playing on a swing teach you something about science? Well, a swing is a *pendulum*. You're going to test whether weight will change the speed of the swing.

I hope this experiment is over before midnight!

You will need:
a watch, outside playground swing, ruler, 2 friends

What to do in this forces experiment

1 Hold the seat of the swing and move back 3 or 4 steps.

2 Ask your friend to put the ruler on the ground in front of your feet.

3 Using the watch, your friend is to start timing when you let go of the swing. Don't push the swing, just let it go. Count the number of times the swing goes back and forth in 10 seconds.

4 Your friend must call out when 10 seconds is up.

5 Ask your other friend to sit in the swing.

6 Pull the swing back until your feet are behind the ruler like the first time.

7 Have your friend start timing when you let go of the swing. Don't push the swing. Count the number of times the swing goes back and forth in the 10 seconds.

What Happens
The number of back and forth swings are the same.

Why
- Gravity pulls on the swing. It makes the swing fall when you let it go.
- The speed during the swing did change. However, the change was the same for each weight.
- The speed was faster as the swing got close to the upright position.
- It slowed as it moved upward where it stopped.
- Pendulums stop at the highest position of their swing before beginning the downward swing regardless of weight.

Fun Fact

In 1656, the Dutch scientist, Christiaan Huygens, made the first pendulum clock. This was much more accurate in measuring time than earlier clocks. Later, he invented the balance wheel and spring assembly, which is still used in watches today!

Mini Quiz
How long does it take the Earth to spin around once?

Mini Answer ✓
It takes the Earth one day (24 hours) to spin around once.

30 Pen Cap Submarine

Rat's Rating

DOWN PERISCOPE...
DIVE...DIVE...DIVE!

How can a submarine sink in the ocean, then rise again and float on top?

You will need:
small clear plastic soda bottle, modeling clay, plastic pen cap, water

What to do in this forces experiment

1 Fill the clean plastic bottle with water.

3 Put the cap in the bottle so that it floats.

2 Put a piece of modeling clay to the arm of a plastic pen cap.

4 Put the lid on the bottle. It must be tight so that air doesn't leak from the bottle.

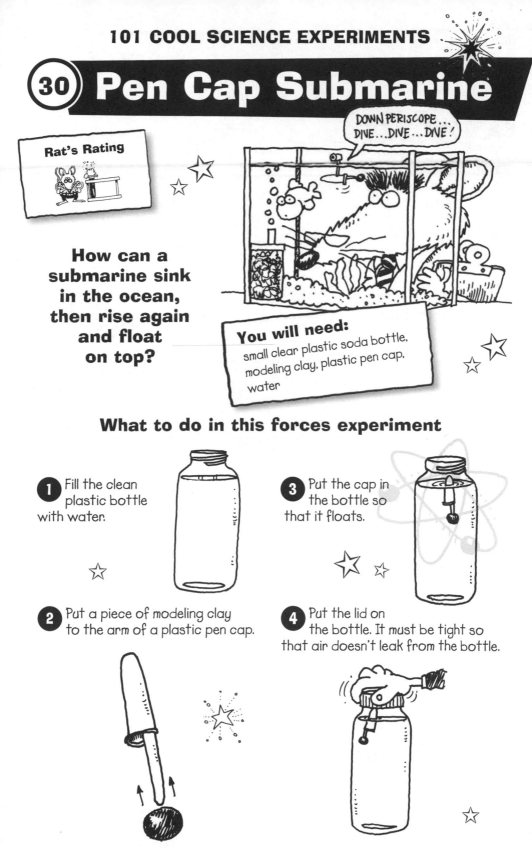

5 Squeeze the sides of the bottle. What do you think will happen?

What Happens
The pen cap sinks when you squeeze the sides of the bottle.

Why
- When you squeeze the bottle, you make more pressure inside.
- This forces more water up into the pen cap.
- The added water in the pen cap makes it weigh more. This makes the cap sink.
- A submarine works in much the same way. Each submarine has tanks that can be filled with water, or air.
- When filled with air, the submarine will float on the surface of the water.
- When the submarine dives, large amounts of water are pumped into the tanks. This makes it much heavier.
- By regulating the amount of water and air in the tanks, the crew of the submarine can make it rise or sink to whatever level they want.

Fun Fact
In the bathtub, pierce a hole in the lid and bottom of a plastic bottle. Push a plastic tube through the hole in the lid. Put your finger over the hole in the bottom. Fill the bottle to the top with water. Screw on the lid. Let the bottle sink to the bottom of the bath. Take your finger away from the hole and blow into the tube.
Your mini-sub will rise to the surface.

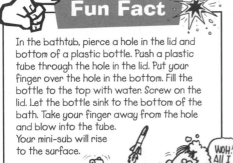

WOH! All I did was fill a plastic bottle full of air!

Mini Quiz
Are submarines a modern invention?

Mini Answer
No! Greeks and Romans wrote about diving bells, and so did medieval writers. An English inventor described a workable submarine in 1578 and a Dutch inventor finally built oar-driven submarines in the early 1600s.

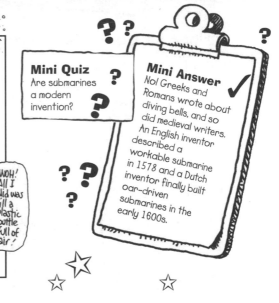

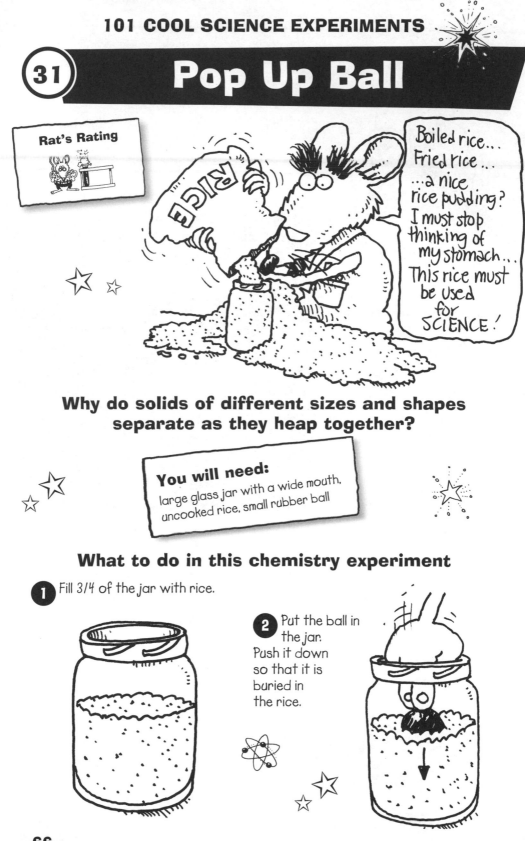

31 Pop Up Ball

Rat's Rating

Boiled rice... Fried rice ... ...a nice rice pudding? I must stop thinking of my stomach... This rice must be used for SCIENCE!

Why do solids of different sizes and shapes separate as they heap together?

You will need:
large glass jar with a wide mouth, uncooked rice, small rubber ball

What to do in this chemistry experiment

1 Fill 3/4 of the jar with rice.

2 Put the ball in the jar. Push it down so that it is buried in the rice.

BALL

3 Place the jar on the table. Shake it back and forth. What will happen to the ball?

What Happens
The ball comes to the top of the jar!

Why
- In any mix of solids there are spaces in-between the pieces.
- When your mix is shaken, the grains rearrange themselves.
- Gravity forces the grains downward.
- The grain needs a space to move into.
- As you shake the jar, each rice grain finds a space. But there is never a space big enough for the ball.
- As the ball moves up, rice grains settle underneath. They stop the ball from moving back down. With each shake, the ball moves up, but not down.
- After a few minutes of shaking the ball comes out from the rice and sits on top.

Fun Fact
You can use mixed nuts to see another example of separation. Shake the can of nuts. Open them. The bigger nuts like Brazil Nuts will be at the top. The smaller nuts will mainly be on the bottom.

Hey sonny... keep shaking that can! It's bringing all my favorite Brazil Nuts to the top!

Mini Quiz
Why is rice thrown at a wedding?

Mini Answer ✓
The custom comes from the ancient Hindus and Chinese. In these cultures, rice is the symbol of success. Today, throwing rice is being replaced by birdseed. This is because uncooked rice hurts the birds that eat it.

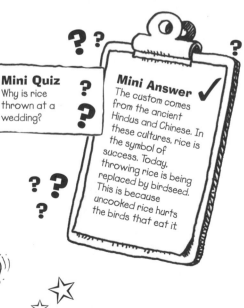

Hot Stuff

32

Kaboom

Rat's Rating

How can water float on water? Make your own underwater volcano and find out.

You will need:
small glass bottle, water, food coloring, string, large glass jar (big enough for the bottle to fit inside), scissors

What to do in this heat experiment

1 Cut a long piece of string. Tie one end tightly around the neck of the bottle.

2 Tie the other end of the string around the neck of the bottle to make a loop.

3 Pour cold water into the large glass jar until it is about 3/4 full.

4 Fill the small glass bottle with hot water.

5 Add food coloring – red looks good!

6 Hold the bottle by the loop of the string.

7 Gently lower it the jar of cold water.

What Happens

The hot red water rises from the bottle like smoke from an erupting volcano.

Why

- The water looks as if it is still, but it isn't!
- Its molecules are always moving.
- Molecules move more quickly when they are hot.
- Hot water always rises to the surface and floats on the cold water.
- Cooler molecules sink.

Fun Fact

The Mid-Ocean Ridge is the biggest mountain range on our planet. It's more than 30,000 miles (48,280 km) long and almost 500 miles (804 km) wide. Nearly every day, at least one underwater volcano erupts.

QUICK! RUN!... I mean SWIM FOR YOUR LIFE! IT'S ABOUT TO BLOW!!

Mini Quiz
How can a volcano erupt underwater?

Mini Answer ✓
An underwater volcano can erupt under water because it is not a fire. Fire is a chemical reaction. It needs oxygen to keep going. If you put a fire under water, you take away the source of oxygen. The chemical reaction stops. Underwater volcanoes are very different. What you see on the surface is material that is already hot. It doesn't need any reaction at the surface to make it hot. There isn't any way for the water to "put out" the eruption. This is because the water is changed to steam, which then explodes.

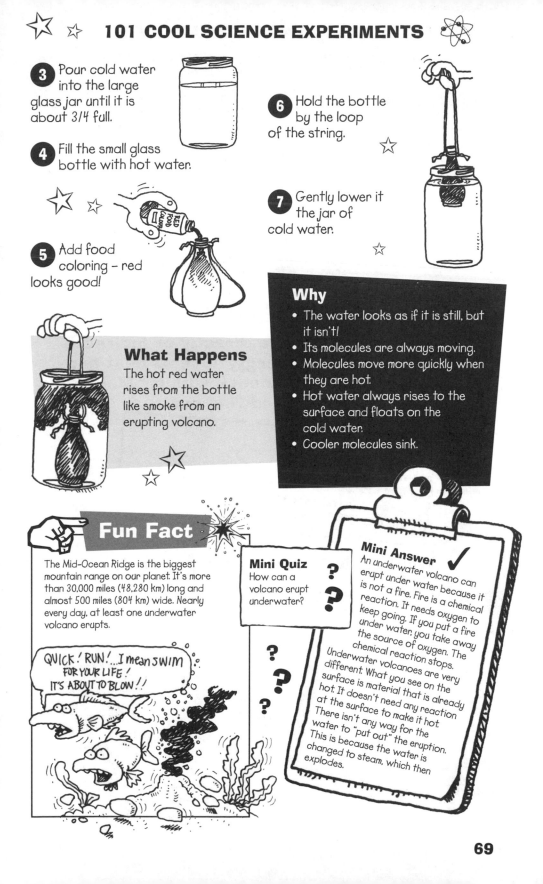

Hot Diggity Dog

33

Rat's Rating

YUM! THERE'S NOTHING LIKE...
.............an empty pizza box!

Solar energy can change directly or indirectly into other forms of energy, such as heat and electricity. But can you cook with it? Make a solar oven and find out.

You will need:

a very hot sunny day, pizza box, black construction paper, wide aluminum foil sheet of plastic, glue, tape, scissors, ruler, marker, string, nail, skewer, choice of food to cook - hot dogs/pancakes

What to do in this heat experiment

1 Tape the foil to the inside bottom of the clean pizza box.

2 Cover the foil with the black paper. Tape it down.

3 Put the box on the sheet of plastic.

4 Draw the outline of the box on the plastic with the marker.

5 Cut the plastic about 1/4 inch (0.5 cm) inside the marks.

CUT 0.5cm in from PEN LINE

6 On the top of the box, draw a line 1 inch (10 cm) from all sides.

7 Cut along the front and side lines. Do not cut along the back. This will be the hinge for the flap. Carefully fold open the flap.

8 Cut a piece of foil the same size as the flap. Glue it to the side of the flap that faces into the box. Flatten out any wrinkles.

FOIL

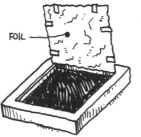

9 Wipe any glue off with a damp towel before it dries.

10 Tape the plastic to the inside of the box. Make it tight so it looks like glass.

TAPE PLASTIC ON HERE

FOIL

11 Tape the other edges. Make sure it is tight so no air can get in.

12 Cut a piece of string as long as the box. Tape one end to the top of the flap.

13 Push a small nail into the back of the box so you have a place to tie the string.

14 Poke a metal skewer through the middle of your hot dog. It will cook more quickly if cut in half.

15 Put the hot dog in your solar oven. Place the oven in a hot spot. The sun needs to shine right into the box. The best time to use your solar oven is between 12 and 2.00 p.m. This is when the sun is at its strongest.

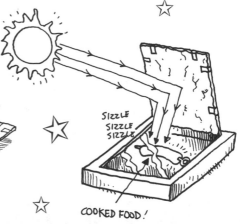

SIZZLE SIZZLE SIZZLE

COOKED FOOD!

What Happens
Your food will cook, but it can take many hours.

Why
• Your hot dog oven is a solar collector. Sunlight hits the reflective foil surface. It focuses on the hot dog held in the center.

34 Steel Wool Wonder

Rat's Rating

After the washing up... I have just the scientific experiment for you my friend!

A chemical reaction is where one type of substance is chemically changed to another substance. The Sun is one big chemical reaction. The fire in your fireplace is another type of chemical reaction. Can you make another?

You will need:
thermometer, clean jar with lid, steel wool scouring pad with no soap inside, pencil, paper, bowl, vinegar

What to do in this temperature experiment

1 Put the thermometer in the jar. Put the lid on.

2 Wait about 5 minutes and write down the temperature.

3 Take the thermometer out of the jar.

4 Put a clean steel wool scouring pad in a small bowl.

5 Pour vinegar over the pad until it is completely covered. Soak it for 1 minute.

6 Lift out the steel wool and squeeze out the vinegar.

7 Wrap the steel wool around the bulb of the thermometer.

8 Place the thermometer and steel wool back in the jar. Put the lid on.

9 Wait 5 minutes then look at the temperature. Will it be up or down?

What Happens

The temperature rises.

Why

- The vinegar takes away any protective coating from the steel wool.
- This causes the iron in the steel to rust.
- Rusting is a slow mix of iron with oxygen.
- When this chemical reaction happens, heat energy is released.
- The heat released by the rusting of the iron makes the mercury in the thermometer expand and rise.

Fun Fact

One ton of iron turns into three tons of rust. This is why the battle to stop rust forming on cars, bridges, and buildings is never-ending!

It's a true bargain!! It might look like 3 tons of rust.... But there's actually 1 ton of car under that!

Mini Quiz
Why do some metals rust and others don't?

Mini Answer
Rust forms only on metals that have iron. It is the result of a chemical reaction between the iron and the moisture and oxygen in the air. Keeping oxygen and moisture from the surface of metal can stop rust.

Make a Thermometer

35

The things a rat will do for science...!

Rat's Rating

This one is to see how a thermometer works — just for fun.

You will need:
clear medicine bottle or very small jar, clear drinking straw or medicine dropper tube, cold water, spoon, food coloring, modeling clay/plasticine, marker, note book paper

What to do for this temperature experiment

1 Pour cold water into the medicine bottle. Fill to about 1/4 full.

2 Add a couple of drops of food coloring.

3 Get a wad of modeling clay. Push the straw through it. Unclog the straw if bits of clay end up in it.

4 Put the straw in the bottle. Make sure it doesn't touch the bottom.

5 Work the modeling clay to seal the neck of the bottle. The straw needs to stay in place.

6 Blow gently into the straw so the water rises. When it is halfway up the straw stop blowing.

7 Use your marker to make a line where the water has risen on the straw.

8 Write down the height of the water in the straw. This will be the height at room temperature.

9 Hold your hands on the bottle. Watch what happens to the height of the mixture in the bottle.

10 Mark the new level with a different color pen.

What Happens

The height of the mixture rises.

NEW LEVEL

OLD LEVEL

Why

- Just like any thermometer, the mixture expands when it becomes warm. This means the liquid no longer fits in the bottom of the bottle.
- As the water expands, the colored mixture moves up through the straw.

Fun Fact

The Italian physicist Galileo invented the first thermometer in 1593.

Mama-Mia it's-a hot in-a here! I should invent-a a THERMOMETER to see-a how hot it is! It's-a like living in-a the tropics!

Mini Quiz
How is temperature measured?

Mini Answer ✓
Temperature is measured on the Fahrenheit scale in the United States and in the Celsius scale in the rest of the world.

36 The Drip

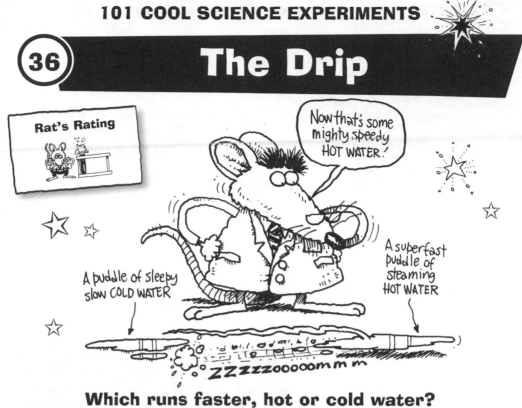

Rat's Rating

Now that's some mighty speedy HOT WATER!

A puddle of sleepy slow COLD WATER

A superfast puddle of steaming HOT WATER

ZZZZZZoooooommm m

**Which runs faster, hot or cold water?
Hot runs faster because you can't catch a hot,
but you can catch a cold!**

You will need:
paper cups, pins, small drinking glass, water, ice-cubes

What to do in this temperature experiment

1 In the middle of the bottom of 2 paper cups make a tiny pinhole. Make sure they are the same size.

2 Stand the paper cups on top of the glasses.

3 Pour very cold water into 1 glass until it's 1/2 full.

4 Add a few ice-cubes to make sure it is really cold.

5 Pour hot water into the other glass until it is also 1/2 full. Watch as water drips from the paper cups into the glasses. Do you see any differences?

What Happens

If the holes are the same size, you'll see that the hot water leaks faster than the cold water. If the cold water is cold enough it may not leak at all.

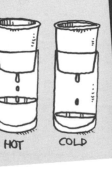

HOT   COLD

Why

- Molecules exist although we can't see them.
- The molecules in hot water move faster than in cold water.
- The faster they move, the easier it is for them to slip past each other. That is why hot water is more likely to leak than cold.

Fun Fact

You can see molecules with the help of food coloring. Get 2 drinking glasses that are exactly the same. Put 1/2 a cup of water in each of them. One glass should have cold tap water and the other hot tap water. Put 2 drops of food coloring in each glass. Time how long it takes for each of the colors to spread in the water. Molecules make the colors spread.

Mini Quiz
What do molecules look like?

Mini Answer ✓
Molecules are so small that it is almost impossible to see them, even with a powerful microscope. But scientists know how to make models of molecules. The models help scientists study how molecules interact.

Pop Goes the Popcorn

37

Rat's Rating

O.K! All I need now is a fizzy drink and a movie... to make this experiment complete!

Why does popcorn pop? Grab an adult to help you find out. This experiment is hot!

You will need:
unpopped popcorn, a medium pan with a clear lid, at least enough popcorn to cover the bottom of the pan, one kernel deep, 1/3 cup of oil for every cup of kernels (don't use butter), stove

What to do in this temperature experiment

1 Put the oil into the pan.

2 Place the pan on the stove.

3 Ask an adult to heat the oil so that it is very hot (if the oil smokes, it is too hot).

4 Test the oil on a couple of kernels. When they pop, add the rest of the corn.

5 Ask an adult to cover the pan and shake it so the oil spreads evenly.

6 Watch the shape and size of the corn kernels as they are heated.

7 When the popping begins to slow, ask an adult to take the pan away from the stovetop. The heated oil will still pop the rest of the kernels.

What Happens

The corn kernels change from small, hard, orange kernels to big, soft, white shapes.

Why

- The tough outside of the unpopped kernel is the *pericarp*. This is the part that often gets stuck between your teeth when you eat popcorn.
- The inside is full of starch. This grows into the white fluffy popcorn.
- The small amount of water inside the kernel makes this happen. As the kernel is heated, the water evaporates. It changes to a gas. The gas grows and pushes hard on the pericarp. It breaks and the starch tissue inside is blown outward.
- The popping noise is the sound of steam escaping and the pericarp breaking.

Fun Fact

The largest box of popcorn in the world was made in London in 2000. The box was 6 x 6 x 12 feet (1.8 x 1.8 x 3.6 meters) and filled with 784 square feet (22.2 square meters) of popcorn. It took 5 hours to fill.

I DON'T CARE WHETHER IT'S A WORLD RECORD OR NOT... It's going to AVALANCHE!

WORLD POPCORN RECORD

Mini Quiz
How did Ancient civilizations make popping corn pop?

Mini Answer ✓
In Peru, popcorn poppers date back to 300 A.D! The poppers were shallow vessels with a hole on the top and a single handle.

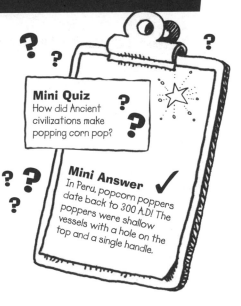

38

Too Twisty Too Twirly

Rat's Rating

How much power do you have in your hot little hands? Find out.

THIS MUST PROVE SOMETHING

ZZZZZZZ

You will need:
adult supervision, thin sheet of paper, pin, pencil with eraser

Rat's Helpful Hint
This experiment works best if your hands are warm and the paper you use is light and very thin.

What to do in this temperature experiment

1 Cut your thin paper into a 3 x 3 inches (7.5 x 7.5 cm) squares.

2 Fold the square diagonally one way and then unfold it.

3 Fold the square diagonally the other way.

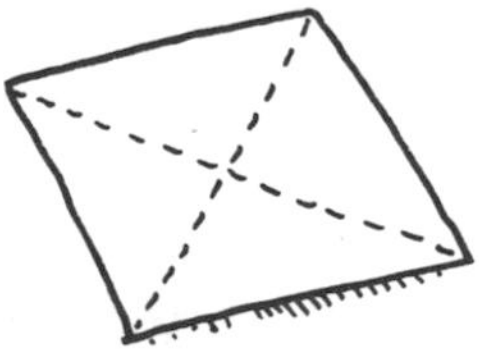

4 Push in gently on opposite sides of the paper. This makes the center rise about 1/2 inch (1.25 cm) higher than the sides.

5 Push the straight pin into the eraser end of the pencil. Leave 1 inch (2.5 cm) of the pin sticking straight up.

6 Sit down and hold the pencil between your knees.

7 Set the paper square on top of the pencil. You must have the head of the pin right at the center peak where the two folds come together.

8 Cup your hands on each side of the paper. They must be about 1 inch (2.5 cm) away from it.

9 Do not move your hands or knees. Wait a minute and watch what happens to the paper.

What Happens

Your paper twirler will begin to turn. Once it gets going your twirler will twirl around and around.

Why

- The warmth from your hands heats the air around them.
- The heated air rises.
- The rising air makes the finely balanced twirler twirl.

Fun Fact

Hot-air balloons don't fly in the rain. This is because balloon heat can cause water to boil on top of the balloon and boiling water destroys the canopy fabric.

ROUND the WORLD ADVENTURE

I bet nobody thought to pack an umbrella?

Mini Quiz
What is your normal body temperature?

Mini Answer
Your normal body temperature is 98.6 degrees Fahrenheit (37 degrees Celsius). If the thermometer shows higher than this, it means you have a fever.

(39) It's Raining Cats and Dogs

Rat's Rating

Fed up with having to water the potted plants? Bring them inside while you do this experiment. You're going to make it rain in your kitchen.

I thought the term 'RAINING CATS AND DOGS' was only just that... ...a term!

WOOF
MEOW
mee-oww
AAHRRR-RUFF

You will need:
saucepan, water, ice-cubes, tray, potholder/oven mitt, an adult's supervision

What to do in this meteorology experiment

1 Put water in the saucepan.

2 Ask an adult to boil the water until steam rises.

3 Hold a tray of ice-cubes above the steam. Use potholders to protect your hands.

4 Keep holding the tray until drops form on the bottom.

What Happens

The drops of water grow heavy and fall like rain.

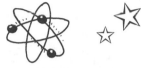

Why

- The cold surfaces of the ice-cube tray cool the steam from the boiling water.
- The steam changes back into water, and collects in drops.
- As the drops get bigger and heavier, it rains.
- The boiling water is like the water that evaporates into the air as water vapor.
- As the vapor rises, it cools. You see clouds when droplets form. As these droplets collect more moisture, they become heavy enough to fall to earth as rain.

Fun Fact

If you hold a piece of cardboard outside when it starts to rain you can measure the size of a raindrop. A downpour has about 113 drops.

A CARDBOARD RAINGAUGE this wet indicates either a SEVERE TROPICAL STORM or a HURRICANE!

Mini Quiz
Which is the wettest place in the world? And don't answer, "In the water."

Mini Answer ✓
Mount Waialeale in Kauai, Hawaii has the highest annual rainfall of 460 inches (1,150 cm).

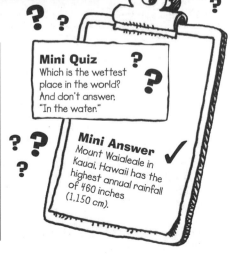

40 Thirty Second Cloud

Rat's Rating

My...! Now that was a quick shower!

Clouds are made when air holding vaporized water cools. Try to make your own cloud inside a jar!

You will need:
large jar with lid, water, white chalk, zip lock plastic bag, round balloon, scissors, thick rubber band

What to do in this meteorology experiment

1 Pour a little water into the jar. Put the lid on tightly. Leave it for 20 minutes.

3 Use your hands to crush the chalk into a powder.

4 Cut off the neck of the balloon.

2 Put white chalk in a zip lock bag. Zip the bag shut.

5 Take off the lid of the jar. Put in the chalk powder.

6 Quickly cover the jar with the balloon.

RUBBER BAND

7 Put a rubber band around the neck of the jar to keep the balloon stretched tight.

8 Press the balloon down with your fist to crush the air. Hold it like this for 30 seconds.

9 Take away the balloon. What do you see?

What Happens

You have made a cloud.

Why

- Cool air can't hold much water vapor. Some of it condenses to make clouds.
- When you compress the air in your jar, the air becomes warmer. It absorbs more vaporized water.
- When you take away the balloon cover, the air cools. Some of the vaporized water condenses on the chalk dust. It makes a cloud.

Fun Fact

Here are the main four groups of clouds and their shapes: cumulus (heap), stratus (layer), cirrus (curl of hair) and nimbus (rain).

A CUMULUS cloud

A STRATUS cloud

A CIRRUS cloud

A NIMBUS cloud

A rather disagreeable cranky STORM cloud!

Mini Quiz
Where does the expression "on cloud nine" come from?

Mini Answer ✓
Being "on cloud nine" means you are very happy. A famous Italian author, Dante, wrote a book about ten steps to heaven. Clouds were used as the steps. Cloud nine was as close to God as you could get.

41 Heat That Rubber!

Rat's Rating

Most materials expand when heated, but some are a little different. Turn a hair dryer on a rubber band and watch what happens.

You will need:
a large rubber band, hair dryer, small light toy such as a plastic action figure, hook or doorknob on which to hang the rubber band, small table

What to do in this heat experiment

1 Attach the toy to one end of the rubber band.

2 Hang the rubber band on the hook or knob so that the toy is hanging down.

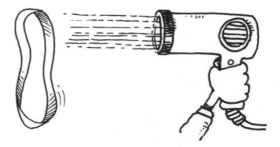

3 Place the table underneath the toy so it is just touching the table.

4 Using the hair dryer, heat the rubber band until it is very warm (this won't take long, so be careful not to melt the rubber band).

5 What is happening to the toy as you heat the rubber band?

What Happens

- As you heat the rubber band, the plastic toy is lifted off the table.
- As the rubber cools again after heating, the toy will be lowered back onto the table.

Why

- Unlike most materials, rubber shrinks when it is heated.
- Rubber molecules move around more when they are heated, and become tangled.

Fun Fact

There are two types of rubber used in the world today.

Natural rubber comes from a liquid called latex, which is harvested from special rubber trees. Synthetic rubber is made from chemicals, many of which come from fossil fuels such as oil and coal.

Mini Quiz
Where do rubber trees grow?

Mini Answer ✔
Rubber trees grow in tropical climates. The first rubber tree plantations were in South America. Today, most rubber trees are grown in South East Asia. Rubber latex is harvested from the trees by making small cuts in their trunks and allowing the sap (which contains latex) to trickle out. This is called "rubber tapping."

Stars in Your Eyes

42 It's Just a Phase

Rat's Rating

I wonder if it is made out of green cheese... ...yum! Makes your mouth water!

Ever been told, "You're just going through a phase?" Well, the moon goes through a phase, too. But it won't grow out of it.

You will need:
2 inch (5 cm) or bigger white Styrofoam ball, lamp with a bright bulb (400 watts), sharp pencil

Rat's Helpful Hint
Make sure no-one's head gets in the way of this experiment, or they will cause a lunar eclipse!

What to do in this astronomy experiment

1 Put the lamp in the center of the room.

2 Take away the lampshade. You only need to see the bulb.

3 Push the foam ball into the sharp end of the pencil.

4 Hold the pencil in your left hand.

5 Place the ball at arm's length between the bulb and your eyes. The bulb is the Sun. The ball is the Moon. You are the Earth!

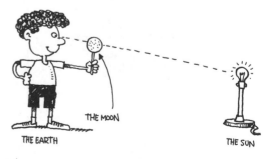

THE MOON

THE EARTH

THE SUN

6 Your ball (Moon) is blocking the bulb (Sun). This is what a total solar eclipse looks like!

Move your ball (Moon) so that you look into the bulb (Sun). Look at your moon. All of the light shines on the far side. This is opposite the side you are looking at. This phase is called the *new moon*.

☆

Move your hand to the left, about 45 degrees of the way around counterclockwise. Look at the light on your Moon. The right hand edge is lit as a crescent. The crescent starts out very thin. It fattens up as the Moon moves farther away from the Sun.

☆

9 When your Moon is at 90 degrees to the left, the right half of the Moon lights up.

10 Keep moving your hand counterclockwise. When the Moon reaches directly opposite the Sun, the part seen from Earth is fully lit. Of course, only half of the Moon is lit. It has taken the Moon about 2 weeks to move from new to full.

11 Switch the pencil to your right hand. Face the lamp Sun.

12 Start with your Moon at full. Keep going on its counterclockwise course. You'll see the opposite phases of the Moon. The Moon will reach the 270° position, straight out to the right. A thinning crescent and a return to new moon follows this.

What Happens
The Moon chases the Sun across the day and night sky.

Why
- From full to new, the Moon has been waning and leading the Sun.
- The phase cycle takes 29.53 days. Why not watch the real Moon? Most newspapers give the Moon phases along with the weather data.

43 Meet a Meteor

WHOA! Will you look at that! A little bit of something ...from somewhere in space!

Meteors are small chunks of broken comets or asteroids. As they enter Earth's atmosphere, they burn up. Find out if this is fact or friction.

You will need:
large soft drink bottle, warm water, seltzer tablet

What to do in this astronomy experiment

1 Fill the bottle with warm tap water.

2 Drop the seltzer tablet into the bottle. Watch what happens.

What Happens

The seltzer tablet breaks up into many small pieces. These disappear as it travels to the bottom of the bottle.

Why

- The water is like the atmosphere of the earth. The tablet is like the meteor.
- Like a meteor, the tablet breaks up into many small pieces as it drops to the bottom of the bottle (the surface of the earth).
- Meteors travel through space at great speeds.
- The force of their surfaces rubs against the atmosphere of the earth. This makes them heat up so much that they break up and explode into space dust.

Mini Quiz
Are there different types of friction?

Mini Answer ✓
There are two main types of friction. These are *static* and *kinetic*. Static friction is the amount of resistance to movement when an object is static, or not moving. Kinetic friction is the resistance on a moving object. Kinetic friction can be sliding or rolling friction.

Fun Fact

Everyday a thousand tons of meteor dust falls on the Earth.

AHHRRR... Meteor dust!

THINGS FROM SPACE

44 Micrometeorites

Perhaps it's a little piece of Pluto!

Rat's Rating

Has a meteor landed in your backyard? Try this experiment. You might be surprised.

You will need:
sheet of white paper, small paint brush, jar, magnet, microscope

What to do in this astronomy experiment

1 Find a place in your house where floating bits of fine particles collect. Window and door screens and the bottom of outside drain spouts work well.

2 Use a brush to collect the particles. Make sure they are dry and put them in a small jar.

3 Shake the particles onto a sheet of white paper. Roll the sides up. Gently tap all the particles into the center of the sheet.

4 Place a magnet under the paper.

5 Gently tilt and tap the paper to get rid of non-magnetic particles. What is left?

What Happens

Some of the left over metallic particles are bits of space dust! To look at them, place the paper under a microscope. You'll need to use high power to see them clearly. The micrometeorites will show signs of their fiery trip through the atmosphere. They will be rounded and may have small pits on their surfaces

WOW! There's a whole METEORITE SHOWER going on here!

Why

- Tons of space dust and debris blast the earth every day.
- Much of what you see are particles that date from when the solar system was formed.
- This is debris left from the raw materials that formed into the nine known planets and the asteroids. This was 4 – 5 billion years ago!
- Most particles have been broken off, or ground down from larger objects.

Fun Fact

Shooting stars are not really stars. They are small bits of rock and metal that hit into the upper atmosphere of Earth. And, because of friction, burn up. Sometimes, man made satellites and spacecraft parts fall into the atmosphere. These burn up the same way.

Well there goes the satellite broadcast of the big match.... because there goes the satellite through the Earth's atmosphere!

Mini Quiz
Why are pieces of rock so important?

Mini Answer ✓
Meteorites are very important for scientists to study. Apart from a small amount of moon rock brought back by the *Apollo* and *Luner* missions, meteorites are the only material evidence that there is a universe beyond the Earth.

Sounds of Science

(45) Straw Oboe

Rat's Rating

Here is your chance to make all the noise you want – and you can blame it all on science.

AHHRR... My favorite OBOE CONCERTO!

We hope that you enjoyed this live performance of the DRINKING STRAW CONCERTO in G MINOR

It sounded like an OBOE to me!

You will need:
drinking straw, scissors ☆

Rat's Helpful Hint

Try this early on a Sunday morning when the rest of the house is asleep. The best way to do it is to stand by a bedroom door. Be careful though, sound bytes bite, so maybe you really shouldn't!

What to do in this Sound experiment

1 Pinch flat 1/2 inch to 3/4 inch (12–19 mm) at one end of the straw.

2 Cut off little triangles. These make the reeds.

3 Put the straw far enough into your mouth so your lips do not touch the corners.

4 Press with your lips on the straw, but not too hard.
Blow gently just past the cut. Listen to the sound. Keep trying. It may take a few tries.

5 Cut three small slits along the length of the straw about 1 inch (2.5 cm) apart.

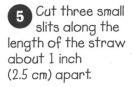

6 Separate the slits so they form small holes.

7 Cover one of them and blow as before.

8 Then cover two, then three, blowing each time. Keep listening.

What Happens

Each time you blow, you hear a different sound. You can play simple tunes by covering and uncovering the holes.

Why

- As in a real oboe, the reeds open and close at high speed.
- This first allows air to flow into the straw and then to stop the flow.
- Vibrating air makes the sound.
- As you cover and uncover the holes, you regulate the length of the air column. That decides the pitch.
- The shorter the air column, the faster it vibrates and the higher the note.

Fun Fact

Another way to be heard is with a piece of cellophane 2 inches (5 cm) square. Stretch it tightly between the thumbs and index fingers of both hands. Hold your hands in front of your face so the cellophane is in front of your lips. Blow hard and fast at the edge of the tightly stretched piece of cellophane. Keep your lips close together. You must send a thin stream of air right at the edge of the cellophane.

Can you hear a noise? When the air hits the edge of the cellophane, you'll make a scream. If you don't, change the distance between the cellophane and your lips until the air hits it just right. The fast moving air from your lip makes the edges of the cellophane vibrate. Because the cellophane is very thin, the jet of air makes these vibrations very fast. The faster something vibrates the higher the tone it creates.

Some parents proudly say their children play the violin... the trumpet... or even ... the drums! We have to say ours plays ... THE CELLOPHANE!

EEEEEEEE EEEEEEEE

Mini Quiz
Which instrument sounds the "tuning note" to which all the instruments of an orchestra, or band, adjust their tuning?

Mini Answer ✔
The oboe sounds the tuning note for the rest of an orchestra. It uses a double reed, which is two pieces of cane tied together.

46 Shake That Salt

Rat's Rating

I could swear that SALT was over there next to the pepper a second ago... ...must be part of this experiment!

Don't you hate it when no one passes you the salt at the dinner table? Let's make salt move without touching it. Is it a mystery? Is it magic? Or is it science?

You will need:
rubber band, piece of plastic, large can, wooden ruler, small can, salt

What to do in this sound experiment

1 Pull the plastic tightly over the open end of the large can.

2 Put the rubber band over it.

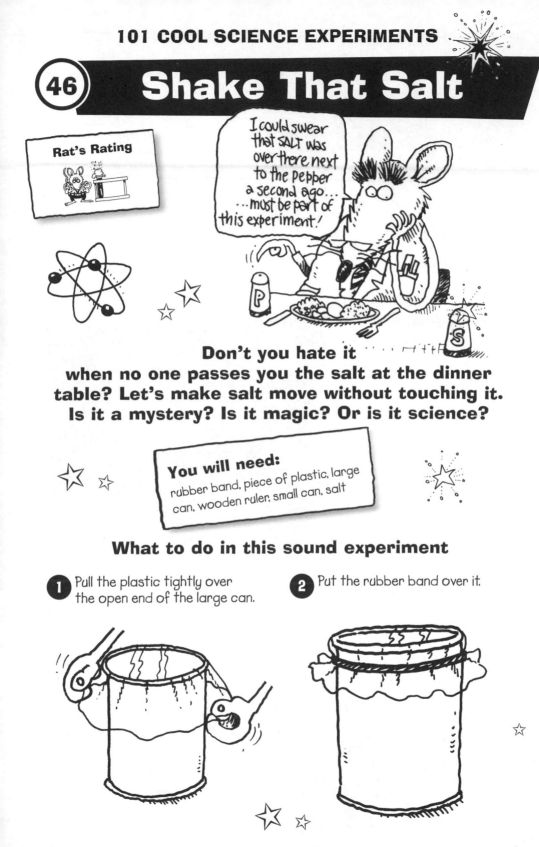

3 Sprinkle some salt on top of the plastic.

4 Hold the small can close to the salt. Tap the side of the small can with the ruler. What do you think will happen to the salt?

What Happens

The salt moves! Tap the small can in different spots or hold it in different directions. Find out how you need to hold and tap the can to get the salt to move the most.

Why

- Sound vibrations travel through the air and when they hit the plastic stretched over the can like a drum, it vibrates.
- This causes the salt to bounce.
- Your ear also has a drum.
- It's called an eardrum and works because of sound vibrations too.

Fun Fact

You can make even the lightest taps of your fingers sound loud. Sit at a table and place your ear flat on the tabletop. Tap with your finger on the surface of the table about 1 foot (30 cm) away from your ear. Tap hard. Then tap softly. The sound of your tapping finger is much louder than when you listen to the same tapping normally. This is because sound waves travel through solids too! Many solids like wood carry sound waves much better than air. This is because the molecules in wood are closer together than those in air.

He says it's part of a scientific experiment...
...but I think it's just an excuse to not eat his BEANS

Mini Quiz
How fast does sound travel?

Mini Answer
Sound travels through the air at about 1,129 feet per second (344 meters). The speed of light travels about 186,000 miles per second (300,000 km). To find out how far away you are from a thunderstorm, count the seconds that pass between seeing the lightning flash and hearing the thunder. Divide the number of seconds by 5 (for miles) or by 3 (for km). So, how far away is the storm?

47 String Orchestra

Rat's Rating

As a child...I practiced playing 'THE STRING' Let's be thankful I took it no further...'

EEEEEE EEEE eeee eeee

String instruments make sounds with vibrating strings. Let's see if you can too.

You will need:
2 pieces of string, paper cup, paper clips, small can, water

What to do in this sound experiment

1 Half fill the small can with water.

2 Tie 1 paper clip to the end of 1 piece of string.

3 Put the other string through the hole in the paper cup.

4 Tie the second paper clip to the end of the string in the paper cup.

5 Hold up the string without the cup, by the paper clip.

6 Wet your fingertips in the can of water.

7 Squeeze the string between your fingertips near the paper clip. Pull your fingers down the string. You should hear a sound.

8 Hold up the cup with the string hanging down.

9 Get your fingers wet again.

10 Squeeze the string and pull your fingers down it. You should hear another sound. What is different about the two sounds?

Why

• Vibrations in the string make the cup vibrate too.
• Since the cup is bigger, it moves more air. This makes a louder sound.
• The same thing happens with instruments like the violin. The vibrating strings make the wood body vibrate. This makes a louder sound.

What Happens

The sound from the cup is louder.

Fun Fact

The vibrating parts of musical instruments don't make sound waves of just one frequency. This is because the string, or forced air, doesn't just vibrate as a whole. Smaller parts also vibrate. In musical instruments, the extra frequencies are called *overtones*. When the overtones are close to the basic frequency, your brain thinks it's a single pitch (level of sound). Different instruments have different strengths of their overtones. This is also what makes your voice sound different from someone else's, even when you sing the exact same pitch.

Mini Quiz
How do you measure sound?

Mini Answer ✓
Sound is measured in decibels (dB) – this is the force of sound waves against the ear. The louder the sound, the more decibels it is. Here are approximate decibel levels for some everyday sounds:

Watch ticking 20
Normal talking 50
Doorbell 80
Baby crying 110
Sporting event 120
Kid's noisy squeeze toy 135
Rock concert 140
Jet engine taking off 150
Fireworks 160
Shotgun fire 170
Rocket launch 180.

OK...OK! Who's singing off key... as well as singing a different song from everyone else?

(48) The Bells! The Bells!

Rat's Rating

The things I'll do for an experiment!

How can a spoon sound like a bell? No, this isn't a riddle. It's science!

You will need:
scissors, string, metal spoons
- teaspoon - soup spoon -
tablespoon/serving spoon

Rat's Helpful Hint
Make sure the spoons are dry.
You don't want to slosh water
all over the floor.

What to do in this sound experiment

1 Cut a piece of string into a 30 inch (75 cm) length.

2 Tie a loop in the middle of the string, but don't pull it into a knot.

3 Put the handle of the teaspoon through the loop. Pull the loop tight so the spoon won't slip out.

4 Move the spoon so that it hangs with the round end just a little lower than the handle.

5 Press one end of the string against the outside of your right ear.

6 Press the other end against the outside of your left ear.

7 Swing the string gently so the curve of the spoon hits the edge of a table. What do you hear?

Hey... groovy sound!

DINK DINK

What Happens

By swinging the spoon gently, you'll hear a bell ring! Repeat the experiment by using a soup spoon and listen to the difference in sound. Now try a tablespoon or serving spoon.

The bigger the size, the deeper the sound.

This must surely be BIG BEN

Why

- The metal in the spoon starts to vibrate when it hits the table.
- The string conducts this vibration.
- The molecules in the spoon move back and forth (vibrate), and hit against each other.
- When molecules hit, energy moves from one molecule to the other.
- The vibrating molecules in the spoon hit against the molecules of the string.
- Not only does string carry sound waves better than air, it sends them right into your ear. This is why you hear the deep sound of bells.

Fun Fact

Indian snake charmers don't play old-fashioned traditional tunes to charm their snakes. Instead, they play popular music from current Indian films!

I'm not even thinking of coming out until you put on the theme from the movie ... "SHE BROKE MY HEART OVER A DISH OF TANDOORI ONE NIGHT IN THE PUNJAB"

Mini Quiz ? How do you hear sound?

Mini Answer ✓ You hear sound because of movement in the air. As the source of a sound vibrates, it moves the air molecules around. These in turn set air molecules around them vibrating, and so the sound is sent through the air to your ears. When the air molecules in your ear start vibrating, your eardrum vibrates. It passes the movement to the inner ear. Nerves then take the information to the brain and you hear sound.

Busybody

(49) It's Snot Fair!

Rat's Rating

Feel left out when your friends are fussed over because they have colds and you don't? Try making your own mucus! It looks just as revolting as the real stuff, but you don't have to get sick.

You will need:
corn syrup/golden syrup, unflavored gelatin, measuring cup, water, microwave oven or stove, green food coloring (optional but it makes the mix look so disgusting), fork

What to do in this anatomy experiment

1 Ask an adult to help you heat 1/2 cup of water until it boils.

2 Take the pan off the heat. Add a tiny drop of food coloring to the water.

3 Sprinkle in 3 envelopes of unflavored gelatin.

4 Let it soften a few minutes and stir with a fork.

5 Add enough corn syrup to make 1 cup of the thick mixture.

6 Stir with a fork and lift out the long strands of gunk.

URRR! Where's my hanky?

7 As it cools, you'll need to add more water, spoonful by spoonful.

Why
- Mucus is mainly made out of sugars and protein. That is what you used to make your fake mucus, only you use different proteins and different sugars.
- Those long, fine strings inside your fake mucus are proteins. They are why real mucus can stretch out quite long.
- The protein helps make it sticky, too. The protein in your fake mucus is gelatin.

What Happens
You have made fake or artificial mucus.

Fun Fact
Put a pinch of fine dust onto your fake mucus. Now stir it up. Look closely into the goo from the side. The fine dust is trapped. That is the why you have mucus in your nose. You use it to trap all the dust, pollen and junk that is floating in the air. With mucus, most of the dirt is trapped and then blown out.

You wouldn't want to see what's in this hankerchief... IT'S THE REAL THING!

Mini Quiz
Your stomach has *hydrochloric acid* inside. This acid is strong enough to eat through a piece of the metal zinc. Why doesn't this eat through you and make you melt?

Mini Answer
The reason your stomach is not destroyed by acid is thanks to mucus. Mucus is thick, sticky, slimy, and gooey, and the inside of your stomach is covered with it. That layer of mucus protects the stomach from its own acid. Your stomach has to make a new layer of mucus every two weeks otherwise it will digest itself.

50 Are You Still Alive?

Rat's Rating

AHHRRR! NO HEART BEAT!

Oh... There it is... HOORAY!! I'M ALIVE...! I'M ALIVE...!

Sound energy travels in all directions, even around corners. Is it possible to catch more of this energy and bring it to one place?

You will need:
piece of garden hose/plastic tube, funnel, a friend

Rat's Helpful Hint
If you want to make your friend jump, rub an ice cube over the end of the tube before using it on their chest.

What to do in this anatomy experiment

1 Push the neck of the funnel into one end of a 3 feet (1 meter) piece of hose. Twist it in tightly so it doesn't fall out. You've just made a stethoscope like the one your doctor uses.

2 Have a friend hold the wide end of the funnel tightly against their chest

3 Put the other end of the hose near your ear. Can you hear your friend's heartbeat?

Can you hear anything?

THUMPA... THUMPA... THUMPA...

4 Let your friend listen to his or her own heart. This means that the hose has to bend, but the sound still follows the hose.

Well you still look alive to me I just can't hear it without that funnel

5 After you've both had a chance to listen to your own and each other's hearts, pull the funnel out of the hose. Try to listen to your friend's heart using just the hose. Can you hear it?

What Happens

You probably can't hear the heartbeat without the funnel.

Why

- The funnel is a cone. It collects a lot of sound energy and concentrates it in the hose. When you use the funnel, a lot more energy reaches your ears. That is, the heartbeat is louder.

Fun Fact

Put a clock on the table. Slowly move your head towards it until you can hear the ticking. Measure how far that is. Take a cardboard tube that is longer than the distance you measured. Hold it to your ear. Can you hear the clock? The sound waves bounce from side to side down the tube and cannot escape into the air.

Sounds like... tick tock... tick tock

Hear anything?

Mini Quiz
Who invented the stethoscope?

Mini Answer ✓
The French doctor Rene Laennec invented the stethoscope in 1819. It was a simple wooden tube one foot long (30cm).

(51) Print Those Fingers

Rat's Rating

Have a look at the tip of your fingers. Look at the grooves in your skin. They make a pattern called a fingerprint. Why not see what your print looks like.

I'd say they were RAT PRINTS! LAB RAT to be precise!

You will need:
ink, inkpad or pencil, sheet of white paper, clear tape, magnifying glass

What to do in this anatomy experiment (using ink)

1. Pour a small amount of ink onto an inkpad. You can also use a saucer with a piece of sponge.

2. Dip your finger into the ink.

3. Lift your finger out.

4. Carefully press your inky finger onto a sheet of white paper.

What to do (using pencil)

1. Using a sharp pencil rub the end across a sheet of paper until you get a layer of *graphite* on the paper.

2 Rub your finger across the graphite on the paper.

3 Tear off about 1 inch (2.5 cm) of clear tape and stick it across the dark end of your finger.

4 Remove the tape and stick it on a sheet of white paper.

LEFT HAND

RIGHT HAND

5 Repeat the process until all of your fingers are fingerprinted. Have a close look at each pattern through a magnifying glass.

Why
- The inner layer of skin is the *dermis*. It has projections.
- The outer layer is the *epidermis*. It fits over these projections and takes on the same pattern.
- These projections are made five months before a baby is born! They never change.

What Happens
The pattern on each fingerprint is the same.

Fun Fact

Fingerprints are very useful for telling who people are. This is because no two people in the world have the same fingerprint. When police try to solve a crime, they use fingerprinting. This means they can see who was at the scene of the crime. They can check these prints with the fingerprints of a suspect.

What sort of thief would play with a stamp pad before he does a job?

One who wants to get caught obviously!

Mini Quiz
Do animals have fingerprints?

Yes, many animals have their own type of fingerprints. The dorsal fins and saddle patches of orcas (whales) are unique for each individual. No two lions have the same pattern of whiskers. No two tigers or zebras have the same pattern of stripes. The fingerprints of koalas are so close to those of humans, that they could be confused at a crime scene!

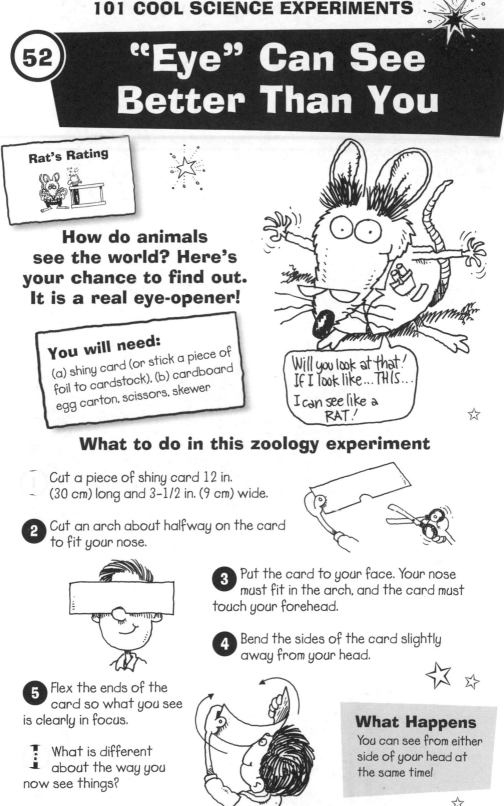

52 # "Eye" Can See Better Than You

Rat's Rating

How do animals see the world? Here's your chance to find out. It is a real eye-opener!

You will need:
(a) shiny card (or stick a piece of foil to cardstock), (b) cardboard egg carton, scissors, skewer

Will you look at that! If I look like... THIS... I can see like a RAT!

What to do in this zoology experiment

1 Cut a piece of shiny card 12 in. (30 cm) long and 3-1/2 in. (9 cm) wide.

2 Cut an arch about halfway on the card to fit your nose.

3 Put the card to your face. Your nose must fit in the arch, and the card must touch your forehead.

4 Bend the sides of the card slightly away from your head.

5 Flex the ends of the card so what you see is clearly in focus.

   What is different about the way you now see things?

What Happens
You can see from either side of your head at the same time!

108

What to do (b)

1 Cut two egg holders from the carton.

☆

2 Using a skewer, make a hole in the bottom of each holder about 1/2 in. (0.5 cm) across. Make sure the holes are a little off center.

HOLE SLIGHTLY TO ONE SIDE

Hey! That's wild!

I feel like some sort of BUG!

3 Put an egg holder over each of your eyes so the holes point in opposite directions.

Why

- The position of an animal's eyes changed over time to suit its needs.
- Our eyes are placed up front. This gives us *binocular* vision and depth perception. This was vital for an animal that once swung through the trees.
- Animals like horses and rabbits have eyes high and to the sides of their head. This lets them see nearly 360 degrees, as well as far above their head. They have a small blind spot directly in front of their face, but forward placed nostrils and big ears make up for that.
- Chameleons see in different directions at the same time. This way they can watch for danger out of one eye and search for food with the other.

What Happens

You can see in two different directions!

Fun Fact

A television screen shows 24 pictures each second. Because a fly sees 200 images each second, a fly watching television sees it as still pictures with darkness in-between. For a fly's eye view, try to flicker your eyelids very fast.

KILLS DEAD FLY FAST SPRAY

NEW

Well...I've had quite enough of that program thank you...I'll be up all night with nightmares!

Mini Quiz
How far can an eagle see?

Mini Answer ✓
An eagle can see a rabbit from about 1 mile (1.6 km) away.

53 Blow a Raspberry

Rat's Rating

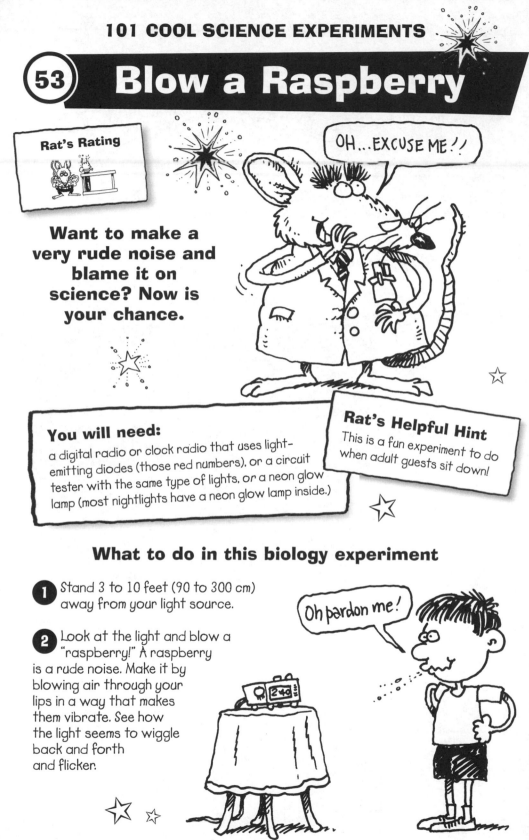

OH...EXCUSE ME!!

Want to make a very rude noise and blame it on science? Now is your chance.

You will need:
a digital radio or clock radio that uses light-emitting diodes (those red numbers), or a circuit tester with the same type of lights, or a neon glow lamp (most nightlights have a neon glow lamp inside.)

Rat's Helpful Hint
This is a fun experiment to do when adult guests sit down!

What to do in this biology experiment

1 Stand 3 to 10 feet (90 to 300 cm) away from your light source.

Oh pardon me!

2 Look at the light and blow a "raspberry!" A raspberry is a rude noise. Make it by blowing air through your lips in a way that makes them vibrate. See how the light seems to wiggle back and forth and flicker.

3 Shake your head quickly. See if the light still flickers. Can you find other body movements that make the light flicker?

What Happens
No part of the light actually moves!

Why

- It is you who actually moves!
- Your whole body is vibrating, even your eyes. You can feel this vibration by putting your hand on your head as you blow.
- The light-emitting diodes flash on and off 60 times per second (a neon glow tube glows on and off 120 times a second).
- This flashing is so fast that your eyes normally can't separate the "blinks".
- When your body is vibrating, your eyes are in a different position each time the bulb flashes.

Fun Fact

Vibrations are everywhere. The building you're in is vibrating a little right now! Earth tremors, traffic, the wind, and people moving make this happen. You're always being hit with vibrations. If you can hear and see, you are using vibrations.

AAHRR... AN EARTHQUAKE

Mini Quiz
Which are the more useful, vibrations from light or sound?

Mini Answer ✓
Both light waves and sound waves are useful in different situations. Light conducts signals much faster than sound. Almost a million times faster! But sound is useful in the dark. It can pass around corners and give information about something out of sight. Light can travel through a vacuum. Sound can pass through materials that would block light. Sound actually travels faster through condensed matter, such as water, than it does through the air.

I am the Walrus

54

Rat's Rating

Under their skin, walruses have a layer of fat. Seals and whales have blubber, too. But is that enough to keep them warm when the temperature is below zero? Try this and see!

You will need:
two cups, cold water, ice cubes, white fat/lard/shortening (the white stuff an adult uses for baking), paper towels

What to do in this anatomy experiment

1 Fill two cups with cold water and ice cubes.

2 Stick one of your fingers in each of the cups. How long can you keep your fingers in there before they get too cold? Now think how a walrus would feel diving into the freezing ocean!

3 Make a ball from a piece of the fat. Put one finger in the middle of it. Make sure the finger is completely covered by the fat.

4 Put the fat covered finger in one of the cups of ice water.

5 Put your other finger in the second cup. Which finger do you want to take out of the cold water first?

What Happens

The fat protects your skin. It stops it from feeling the cold.

I CAN'T STAND THE COLD ANY LONGER!

Why

- Like whales and seals, walruses insulate their bodies with a thick layer of fat called *blubber*.
- A walrus can change the flow of its blood to adjust its body temperature.
- If a walrus gets too hot, its blood rushes to the blubber and skin. It is cooled by the air or water.
- When a walrus is cold, it can reduce the blood flow to its skin and blubber to save heat.

Fun Fact

Cold water, less than 70 degrees F (21 Degrees C), can lower your body temperature. If your body temperature goes too low when you swim, you may pass out and drown. Your body can cool down 25 times faster in cold water than in air. Long-distance swimmers coat their bodies in fats. A diver's wetsuit gives the same thermal protection as blubber.

You just look adorable in all that fat! Are you going my way?

Mini Quiz
Does eating blubber keep you warm?

Mini Answer ✓
People living in Arctic areas eat blubber and other fatty foods. The blubber is taken from marine mammals. Eating blubber helps to build and keep a layer of fat of their own.

(55) Escape a Snake

Rat's Rating

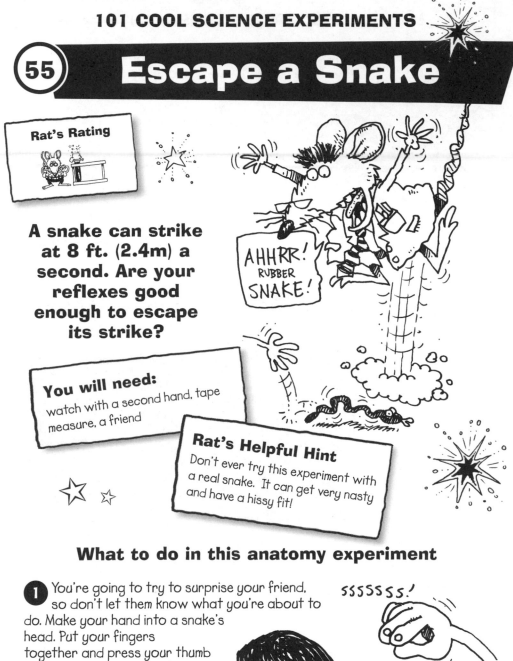

A snake can strike at 8 ft. (2.4m) a second. Are your reflexes good enough to escape its strike?

AHHRR! RUBBER SNAKE!

You will need:
watch with a second hand, tape measure, a friend

Rat's Helpful Hint
Don't ever try this experiment with a real snake. It can get very nasty and have a hissy fit!

What to do in this anatomy experiment

1 You're going to try to surprise your friend, so don't let them know what you're about to do. Make your hand into a snake's head. Put your fingers together and press your thumb against the underside of your first two fingers.

SSSSSS!

2 Pull your hand back as far as it can go toward your shoulder.

"Hey... who are you supposed to be? Cleopatra?"

3 Go up to your friend and stand at arm's length back from them.

4 Get their attention. You need them to face you.

"AAAHHHRRR! A DEATH ADDER!"

HISSSSSSS

5 Dart your hand forwards until your arm is stretched out. What does your friend do?.

Why
- The brain and the rest of the nervous system controls movement.
- Most of the movements you make are under your control. But some are not. These are *reflex actions*.
- A reflex action is an automatic response. Reflexes protect the body. They do this without you having to think about what is happening.
- Reflexes attempt to get you away from objects that could hurt you.

What Happens
Some people will twitch, pull or step back, put their hands up, or blink.

Fun Fact
The average person blinks about 12 times each minute. If you are awake for 16 hours a day, that's about 11,520 blinks per day!

"What a great photo of us all... BLINKING!"

Mini Quiz How does a doctor test your reflexes?

Mini Answer The doctor taps your knee! Your leg kicks out automatically if tapped in the right place. Try it. Have a friend sit with their legs crossed so that one leg can swing freely. Hit the leg just below the knee with the side of your hand. Information is sent to the spinal cord. The tap below the knee makes the thigh muscle contract and the leg kicks out.

56 Brain Pattern

Rat's Rating

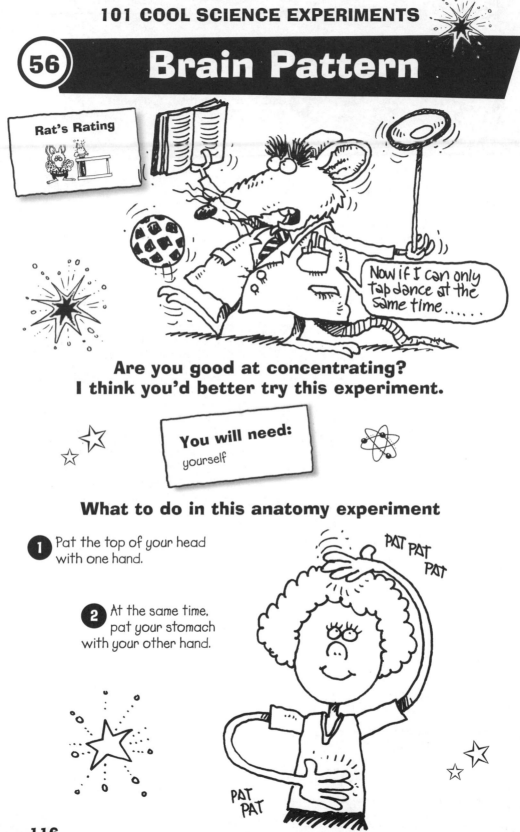

Now if I can only tap dance at the same time......

Are you good at concentrating?
I think you'd better try this experiment.

You will need:
yourself

What to do in this anatomy experiment

1 Pat the top of your head with one hand.

2 At the same time, pat your stomach with your other hand.

PAT PAT PAT

PAT PAT

3 Keep patting your head, but start to rub your stomach in a circle movement.

PAT PAT

4 Swap over. Now, rub your head while patting your stomach.

PAT PAT

What Happens

It is easy for the hands to do the same pattern of movement. But it is hard to do two different movements at the same time.

Why

- When you repeat the same movement, you get used to moving your hands in the same pattern. Your brain is programmed to do this.
- Back and forth movements or circular patterns are easy to do, but only one pattern at a time. Both types of movement are programmed into the brain.
- It takes much more concentration to do two programs at the same time.

Fun Fact

Your brain has a special clock inside. It tells you when to sleep and when to wake up. Without it you'd be waking and sleeping all through the day. The clock is an actual cluster of *neurons*. These send nerve impulses to the brain. The impulses tell us that it is time to go to bed and eight hours later they tell us to wake up.

TICK TICK
TICK TICK
TICK TICK TICK
TICK
TICK

It sounds like someone's brain is ticking!

Mini Quiz
If you have a big brain, are you more intelligent than someone with a small brain?

Mini Answer ✓
There is no direct link between being smart and having a big brain. For example, a larger brain is necessary to control muscles in larger animals. The adult human brain weighs about 3 pounds (1.3 kg). The brain of an elephant weighs up to 20 pounds (6 kg).

(57) You're Rubbing Me the Wrong Way

Rat's Rating

Leaning on the lab bench all day is giving me rough dry elbows... a bit of this scientific sandpaper should do the trick!

Your skin protects your organs. But if you shed skin, why don't your insides fall out?

You will need:
bar of soap, rough sandpaper, sheet of dark paper

What to do in this anatomy experiment

1 Hold the bar of soap over the paper.

2 Gently rub the soap with the sandpaper.

Why

- There are two main layers to your skin. The epidermis (the outer, thinner layers of skin) and the dermis (the inner, thicker layers of skin).
- Nails and toenails sprout out of your epidermis.
- Hair follicles, nerve endings, and glands have their roots in the dermis.
- The epidermis layers rub off by constant rubbing, scratching, and cutting.
- The skin is made of dead cells. These fall off when touched. But your body doesn't wear away like the soap. The layers of epidermis cells are constantly being replaced.

What Happens

The outer surface of the soap is rubbed off by the rough surface of the sandpaper. This is the way the outer layer of your skin is rubbed away by rough objects.

Fun Fact

Every one to three months a snake sheds it skin. Shedding takes only a few minutes once the old skin is rubbed loose at the lips.

By the look of this old skin there's a baby Anaconda living close by . . . .

Mini Quiz
What is the largest organ of the body?

Mini Answer ✔
The skin is the largest organ of the body! You have about 19 million skin cells on every square inch of your body (3 million per square cm). Your skin weighs about 6 pounds (3 kilograms).

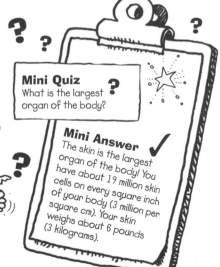

58 Check Your Pulse is True Not False

Where does a RAT check for its pulse?

I must have one!

Maybe it's here...

Your heart beats about 100,000 times in one day and about 35 million times in a year. During your life, it will beat more than 2.5 billion times! Want to check if yours is still going?

You will need:
yourself, clock or watch with a second hand

What to do in this anatomy experiment

1 Take two fingers, the 2nd and 3rd finger work best, and place them in the groove in the wrist that lies under the thumb.

2 Move your fingers back and forth gently. What can you feel?

3 Take the same two fingers and run them alongside the outer edge of your windpipe. What can you feel this time? In both cases, you will feel a slight throb. Do you know why this is?

TRY HERE

What Happens

The throb you feel is your pulse. It throbs as blood moves through your arteries. The first pulse is that of the *radial artery*. It takes blood to the hand. The second pulse is that of the *carotid artery*. It takes blood to the brain, head, and neck. Count the throbs. How many do you count in 15 seconds? Time yourself, or have someone count 15 seconds for you. Multiply your total by 4 and you'll know your pulse rate in beats per minute. Your resting pulse will range from 90–120 beats per minute. An adult has a pulse of about 72 beats a minute. Hummingbirds have an average heart rate of 1,260 beats a minute!

Why

- The pulse represents the beating of the heart.
- As your heart contracts, blood is forced through your blood vessels.
- The blood moves at a rhythmic rate based on your heartbeat.
- This causes the blood vessels in your wrist and neck, and other spots, to pulsate.
- All blood vessels have this throbbing movement.
- The vessels in the wrist are close to the surface of the skin. They are felt more easily.

Fun Fact

You can watch your heart beat. Dim the lights. Lie on your back with your feet pointing towards a wall. Turn on the flashlight. Put it on your chest with the light end resting on the upper, left side of your chest and the beam shining on the wall by your feet. As you watch the beam, it will move up and down as your heart beats.

Want to speed up your heart a bit? Stand up and run in place for a minute. Lie down again and put the flashlight back in place. Do you notice a difference? Exercise means that your muscles need more oxygen. Your heart must pump more blood through your lungs, and then pump it out to your muscles. Your heart beats faster and harder, to pump more blood. If you keep watching, you'll see your heart rate slow back down as your body catches up on its supply of oxygen.

Mini Quiz
How much blood does your body have?

Mini Answer ✓
Your body has about 6 quarts (5.6 litres) of blood. The blood travels through your body 3 times every minute. In one day, the blood travels a total of 12,000 miles (19,000 km). That's four times the distance across America from coast to coast.

Wet Wet Wet

(59) Water Wall

Rat's Rating

IT'S GREAT TO OCCASIONALLY STEP OUT OF THE LAB INTO THE FIELD TO WORK THROUGH EXPERIMENTS ...I THINK!

A *tsunami* (soo-nam-ee) is the Japanese word for "harbor wave". It's a series of traveling waves made by an earthquake below the ocean floor. The waves may even have enough energy to travel across a whole ocean. Tsunamis get higher when they near shallow water. See if you can make your own water wall.

You will need:
deep baking pan, water, blocks of wood ☆

Rat's Helpful Hint
Want to see an adult explode? No? Then you better do it outside and on a warm day.

What to do in this forces experiment

1 Fill the pan with water.

2 Place two blocks of wood in the bottom of the pan. They must be completely below the surface of the water.

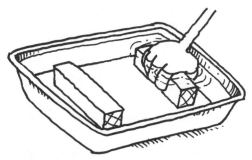

3 Hold the blocks and quickly bring them together.

4 Do it again and again.

5 Continue the squeezing action until the blocks can no longer squeeze the water.

What Happens

The movements of the blocks coming together quickly under the water forces swells of water to the surface. These make waves that splash over the sides of the pan.

Why

- The action of the blocks and the water is like the conditions in the ocean that makes a tsunami.
- On the ocean floor, earthquakes and volcanic eruptions affect the water. They squeeze together big amounts of water and push it to the surface.
- On the surface they make great walls of water.

Fun Fact

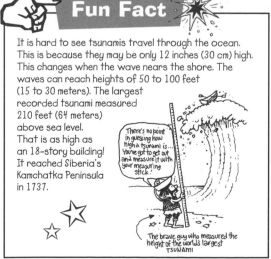

It is hard to see tsunamis travel through the ocean. This is because they may be only 12 inches (30 cm) high. This changes when the wave nears the shore. The waves can reach heights of 50 to 100 feet (15 to 30 meters). The largest recorded tsunami measured 210 feet (64 meters) above sea level. That is as high as an 18-story building! It reached Siberia's Kamchatka Peninsula in 1737.

There's no point in guessing how high a tsunami is... you've got to get out and measure it with your measuring stick!

The brave guy who measured the height of the world's largest TSUNAMI

Mini Quiz
How fast can a tsunami travel?

Mini Answer
A tsunami can move as fast as 500 miles (804 km) per hour.

60 Wave in a Bottle

Rat's Rating ☆

Want to control a tiny ocean? With this experiment, you can see how an ocean wave is made and grows larger. You can have a calm day, or whip up a storm at sea.

You will need:
empty soda bottle and cap (or cork to fit the bottle), vegetable oil, water, food coloring

Rat's Helpful Hint
Make sure you use a clear bottle or you won't be able to see anything!

What to do in this forces experiment

1 Wash out the bottle.

2 Take off the label by soaking the bottle in hot water.

3 Fill the bottle with 3/4 cup of water.

4 Add drops of food coloring. Stop when you like the color.

5 Pour a 1/4 cup of oil into the bottle.

6 Screw on the cap.

7 Turn the bottle on its side. Let it settle for a few minutes. What happens to the water?

What Happens

The water sinks to the bottom. There is a clear line between the colored water and the oil. Now, tip the bottle back and forth and make some waves. Experiment to see what kind of waves you can make. See how the waves grow bigger from one end of the bottle to the other.

Why

- Your bottle wave is like an ocean wave.
- Water moves up and down. It doesn't move forward as the wave goes through the water.
- The friction between the water and the wind makes a wave. They move forward without replacing any water.
- Ordinary ocean waves get their energy from the wind. Higher waves need more energy.
- Wind generated ocean waves keep on traveling after the wind stops.
- Longer waves travel faster than shorter ones and go farther before friction makes them disappear.

Fun Fact

Can a rope be like a wave? Yes, it can! Get a friend to hold one end of the rope, or tie it to a tree. When you shake your end of the rope, waves run along it. But the rope itself doesn't move forward. When an ocean wave reaches land, however, the wave starts to drag on the bottom, and the water begins to move.

AHHRR! RUN! A TIDAL ROPE!

Mini Quiz What makes a wave all foamy?

Mini Answer ✓
Sea foam makes waves look foamy. For sea to foam, it needs two ingredients. It needs something to make the surface tension of the water bigger, like bubble bath. It also needs something to froth it up, like water running into the bath. In the ocean, the "bubble bath" is usually dissolved organic material. Strong surface winds or waves breaking on the beach stirs up the water with air to make bubbles.

61 # Hubble Bubble

Rat's Rating

This experiment started off as me washing my coffee cup

Bubbles are a great way to explore science. Let's see how.

☆

You will need:
plastic cup, bubble blower, bubble mix (store bought or homemade), plastic drinking straw, loop of wire made from a coat hanger, or pipe cleaner

Rat's Helpful Hint
Bubble mix is easy to make from dishwashing liquid. Make sure an adult is supervising . Gently mix 1 part detergent to 8-10 parts of warm water. For example, 1 tablespoon (15 ml) of detergent for every 1/2 cup (125 ml) of water. More detergent than water makes bigger bubbles. Your bubbles will last longer if you let the mix stand for 1–2 days before use. With store bought bubble mix, put it in the refrigerator for a few minutes before using it.

☆

What to do in this water experiment

1 Turn the plastic cup upside down.

2 Wet the bottom of the cup, which is now on top.

3 Use the wire loop to make a large bubble. Attach it to the wet plastic cup.

☆ ☆

4 Wet the plastic straw in the bubble mix.

5 Gently push it through the large bubble.

6 Blow a smaller bubble inside the large one.

7 Carefully push the straw through the smaller bubble and blow an even smaller bubble.

What Happens

You get a bubble in a bubble in a bubble.

Why

- Bubbles are bits of air or gas trapped inside a liquid ball.
- The surface of a bubble is very thin.
- Bubbles are very fragile when a dry object touches them. That is because soap film sticks to the object, which puts a strain on the bubble.
- Anything wet can enter the bubble without breaking it.
- The wet surface meeting the soapy film becomes part of it.
- If you want your bubbles to last longer, keep everything wet, even the sides of the straw. Don't touch the wet wall with your smaller bubble. If you do, you won't get a separate bubble.

Fun Fact

The biggest reported bubblegum bubble in the world was blown in New York City in 1994. The bubble was 23 inches (58.4 cm) wide.

15 seconds after the WORLD'S BIGGEST BUBBLE GUM BUBBLE RECORD was blown

Mini Quiz

What have bubbles got in common with honeycomb?

Mini Answer ✓

Get two sheets of clear plastic. Separate them by a finger and soak them in soapy water. Then blow bubbles between the sheets. You'll get many bubble walls. If your bubbles are of the same size, you'll see that they make hexagons and look like the cells of a beehive. Bees, like bubbles, try to be as efficient as possible when making the comb. They want to use the minimum possible amount of wax to get the job done.

62 Dry Water

Rat's Rating

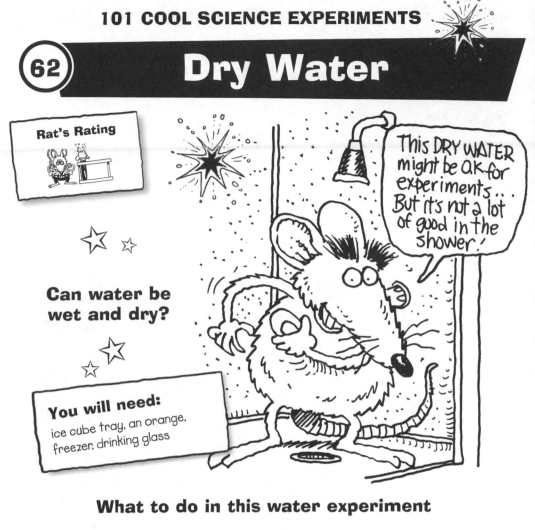

This DRY WATER might be o.k. for experiments... But it's not a lot of good in the shower!

Can water be wet and dry?

You will need:
ice cube tray, an orange, freezer, drinking glass

What to do in this water experiment

1 Squeeze the fresh orange to make juice. Strain if you want.

2 Carefully pour the juice into the ice cube tray.

3 Place the tray in a freezer. Wait a few hours and take the tray out of the freezer.

What Happens
You have made water dry!

Why
- Water can be wet or dry.
- Liquid water is wet, but water is not always liquid.
- Your orange has water inside it. The juice is water that has frozen into ice. Water freezes at 32 degrees Fahrenheit (0 degrees Centigrade).

Fun Fact
Ice cream first came from China in about 200 B.C. It was made from a mix of soft milk and rice. The mix became more solid by packing it in snow.

I'll have a TANG DYNASTY LEMONADE with that GREAT WALL DOUBLE VANILLA CONE ...oh and throw on some GINGER SPRINKLES while you're at it thanks!

Mini Quiz
What is dry ice?

Mini Answer ✓
Dry ice is frozen carbon dioxide (CO_2). We exhale this gas as we breathe. It is much denser (packed tightly together) and colder than normal ice. Dry Ice is -109.3°F (-79.5°C). Normal ice is 32°F (0 degrees C). Dry ice doesn't melt - it goes straight from a solid to a gas – skipping the liquid form, giving it the name, "dry ice".

(63) Paperclip Overboard

Rat's Rating

FLOATING PAPERCLIPS...
now that's handy....
...for something!

FLOATING PAPER-CLIPS

A paperclip floating? Impossible you say.
Try it out!

You will need:
bowl, water, paperclips, tissue paper, pencil with eraser

Rat's Helpful Hint
Don't cheat by putting your paperclip in a little boat to help it float.

What to do in this water experiment

1 Fill the bowl with water.

2 Put the clean paperclip on top of the water. Try to make it float.

3 Tear a piece of tissue paper about half the size of a dollar.

4 Gently drop the tissue paper flat onto the surface of the water.

6 Use the eraser end of the pencil to carefully push the tissue (not the paperclip) until the tissue sinks. What will happen to the paperclip?

5 Carefully place a dry paperclip flat onto the tissue paper. Try not to touch the water or the paper.

What Happens

The paperclip stays afloat!

Why

- Surface tension keeps the paperclip floating. It's like a layer of skin on the surface of water.
- The water molecules hold tight together. If the conditions are right, they can hold tight enough to support the paperclip.
- If you want to make the surface of the water even stronger, try sprinkling some baby powder on it.

Fun Fact

Rub a few drops of cooking oil on your hand. Let water from a tap run over your hand. Turn off the tap. What happens? Now, wash your hands with soap. Does this make the oil go away? The water molecules stick together tightly. They won't mix with the oil on your hand. Soap molecules are attracted to both water and oil. One end of the soap molecule sticks to oil. The other end sticks to water.

The soap breaks up the surface tension. It keeps the oil drops mixed in with the water so that the oil can be washed off your hand.

I'm sure Mom won't mind me using all of her hand soap... It's all in the name of Science!

Mini Quiz
How strong is the surface tension of water?

Mini Answer ✓
Surface tension is strong enough to hold water striders and other insects as they walk on water without sinking. The insects' feet make dents in the surface tension, but the surface tension doesn't break.

Moving Water

This water is going to move.... I just haven't worked out how yet! That's the EXPERIMENT

Do hot and cold water mix?

You will need:
clear jars the same size - baby food jars work well, food coloring red and blue look good, card to fit over the mouth of your jar, water, sink, a friend

What to do in this water experiment

1 Pour cold water and a few drops of blue coloring into jar 1. Slowly add more water until you see a bulge of water over the rim of the jar.

2 Ask an adult to boil some water. Have them fill jar 2 with hot water.

3 Put a few drops of red food coloring into jar 2.

4 Lay the card carefully onto the top of jar 1.

5 This part is tricky. You may want to do it over a sink! Pick up jar 1. Turn it upside down. Put it over jar 2. You want the card to be flat and make a seal. You don't need to put your hand on the card. The water will hold it in place. Just flip the jar over. Don't stop for a second! If the jar tilts, but isn't turned over completely, the water will gush out.

6 Keep the necks of the jars close together. Ask a friend to hold onto both jars while you very slowly and carefully pull out the card. What happens? What color is the cold water in the top jar? What color is the hot water in the bottom jar?

7 Empty both jars. Rinse them. Repeat steps 1 through 6, but put the jar with the cold water in the sink and put the card on top of the jar with the red colored hot water. Turn the hot water jar upside down and put it on top of the cold water jar. What happens? What color is the water in the top jar? What color is the water in the bottom jar?

HOT (RED) RISES INTO THE BLUE

What Happens
The red colored hot water rises into the cold water jar.

Why

- Cold water is heavier than hot water.
- The cold water goes down into the bottom jar pushing the hot water up in small currents.
- When you heat up water, the water molecules start moving around faster and faster. They bounce off each other and move further apart.
- Because there is more space between the molecules, a volume of hot water has fewer molecules in it. It weighs a bit less than the same volume of cold water. So hot water is less dense than cold water.
- When you put the two jars together with the hot water on the bottom, the hot water rises to the top.
- Along the way, it mixes with the cold water and makes purple water.
- When the cold water is on the bottom, the water does not mix. The hot water does not have to rise – it is already on top!

Fun Fact

Would you spend $100 for a glass of water? In America around 1848, people on the way west to the California gold rush did. Because of poor planning, many people weren't ready for the hot, dry deserts of Nevada. A few men in California knew this and traveled east with barrels of water. Very thirsty people paid up to $100 for a glass of precious water.

What'll it be partner? The SPIT ON A ROCK is quite popular!

Unfortunately I've left my credit card back home!

Dusty Gulch INN
SPIT ON A ROCK ~ $15
GLASS WATER $100
BARREL~WATER Credit Card only

Mini Quiz
What Australian animal doesn't drink water.

Mini Answer ✓
The koala! The name koala comes from the native Australian word for "no drink." Koalas get the water they need from eating eucalyptus leaves.

Eat Your Science

65 Baked Ice Cream

Rat's Rating

BAKED ICE CREAM...
Like Mom used to make! This is not baked ice cream... This is melted ice cream! Mum must have had the secret scientific recipe!

Have you ever wondered how ice cream can be baked without melting? Try it and see.

You will need:
eggs, cream of tartar, salt, vanilla essence/extract, measuring spoons, castor/fine sugar, packet of big cookies (chocolate chip are good!), ice cream, oven, cookie sheet, parchment paper, ice cream scoop, egg whisk, bowl

What to do in this chemistry experiment

1 You will need adult supervision. Let 3 eggs come to room temperature.

2 Separate the whites of the eggs from the yolks.

3 Put the egg whites in a bowl.

4 Add 1/4 teaspoon cream of tartar, 1/4 teaspoon salt, and 1/2 teaspoon vanilla extract.

5 Whisk the mixture until it stands up in stiff peaks.

6 Slowly add 1 cup of sugar by sprinkling a tablespoon at a time over the mixture.

7 Continue to stir until the meringue mixture is thick and glossy.

8 Cover the cookie sheet with parchment paper.

9 Put the cookies on the cookie sheet. Leave gaps between them.

10 Place a small scoop of ice cream on each cookie. Keep the ice cream away from the edges of the cookies.

11 Spoon the meringue mixture over the ice cream. You must make sure the ice cream is covered completely by the meringue.

MERINGUE

ICE CREAM

12 Ask an adult to bake the meringues on the bottom rack of a cool oven 225 degrees Fahrenheit (110°C) for about 1 hour. Make sure the meringues don't get brown.

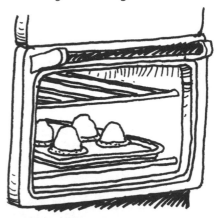

What Happens

The warm oven cooks the meringues, but the ice cream doesn't melt!

ICE CREAM

Why

- Cream of tartar is an acid. When it becomes moist, it releases carbon dioxide. This helps to aerate the meringue.
- When egg whites are beaten, they too make small air spaces.
- Both the air and carbon dioxide are trapped in the beaten egg white. They act as an insulator. As the sugar cooks it hardens. It also acts as an insulator.
- Insulation has small air spaces trapped in it. These slow the movement of heat or cold.
- When the meringue is spread over ice cream, the ice cream is insulated. The heat of the oven can't get in during the baking. Insulation lets the meringue cook without melting the ice cream.

66 Cheese Fractures

Rat's Rating

This is JUST the experiment for a hungry rat

I like cheese sliced...diced ...grated... crumbled... even fractured!

Want to play with your food without being yelled at? Here's your chance. Grab slices of cheese and learn how fractures, breaks and cracks grow.

You will need:
cheese slices (the smooth type that comes individually wrapped in plastic)

What to do in this forces experiment

1 Take a slice of cheese and pull on the edges. Does it tear apart? Good, now eat it.

2 Get another cheese slice. Use your fingernail to make a cut parallel to the edge of the cheese slice.

3 Pull on the edges of the cheese parallel to the cut. You'll be pulling at right angles to the cut. Watch how the small cut you've made in the cheese slice concentrates the tearing. Look at the shape of the fracture. It multiplies at the tips where the tearing is taking place. The fracture tips move faster as the fracture gets bigger. Eat the torn slice.

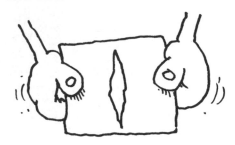

4 Get another cheese slice. Make two cuts near the middle of the cheese about 1 inch (2.5 cm) apart. Make the cuts so they're balanced diagonally from each other.

5 Pull on the cheese. What happens?

What Happens

You have made a fault. This is where things come apart. The tips of these faults begin to multiply and curve inward and link into a single fault line. Like your slice of cheese, basic forces can push or pull on the crusts of the Earth and other planets. This makes tension fractures. Some of these link together to make bigger faults.

Why

- When you pulled on the cheese, you create tension stress throughout the cheese.
- If there's a cut, the stress can't be sent across that fault. Instead, it concentrates around the edges of the fault.
- This concentration of stress means that the cheese wants to split apart around the edges of the cut.
- The bigger the fracture gets, the more stress will be concentrated at the tip of the fracture. This is why it gets easier to pull on the cheese as the fracture grows.
- When the tips of two fractures go past each other, the direction of the stress changes. This is because the stress can't be sent in a straight line across that gap; the fracture tips curve it around. This is what makes the fractures bend toward each other and link up into a larger one.

Fun Fact

Tension fractures often appear as cracks in the surface of a sidewalk, or road. If you look at these cracks, you'll find patterns of cracks like the ones you made in the cheese.

Mini Quiz
Why do earthquakes happen?

Mini Answer
Earthquakes are the Earth's way of releasing stress. When the Earth's plates move against each other, stress is put on the crust. Seismic waves are created when two sides of a fault release this stored up stress by breaking or shifting. When the break occurs, the stress is released as energy, which moves through the Earth in the form of waves, which we feel and call an earthquake

What's the hold-up?

I think there's TENSION FRACTURES in the cheese up ahead

67 Yeast Feast

I should have called this experiment – "OUT TO LUNCH!"

Can a loaf of bread be like a scientific experiment? It can be.

You will need:
full cream milk, unsalted butter, salt, dry yeast, white sugar, water, egg, plain flour, oil, saucepan, small and large bowl, measuring cup, measuring spoons

What to do in this chemistry experiment

1 Pour 2 cups of milk into a small saucepan. Ask an adult to heat the milk until it bubbles. Take the pan off the heat.

2 Add 1/2 cup unsalted butter, 1 teaspoon salt and 2 tablespoons of sugar to the mix. Stir until melted. Let the mix cool until it's lukewarm.

3 Put 2/3 cup warm water into a small bowl. Add 1 tablespoon of active dry yeast. Leave until creamy, about 10 minutes.

4 Pour the milk and yeast mixture into a large bowl. Beat in the egg and add to 3 cups of flour.

5 Stir in the remaining 4 cups of flour a bit at a time. Beat well after each addition.

6 Turn the dough onto a lightly floured surface. Knead until smooth and elastic, about 5 minutes.

7 Lightly grease a large bowl with oil. Put in the dough. Turn to coat with oil.

8 Cover with a warm damp cloth. Let the dough rise about 1 hour in a warm place until twice its size.

9 Punch the dough with your fist. Turn it out onto a lightly floured surface.

10 Divide the dough into 2 pieces. Shape it into loaves.

11 Lightly grease two 9 x 5 inch (22.8 x 12.7 cm) loaf tins.

12 Cover the loaves with a damp cloth. Put them in a warm place. Let them rise for 1 hour until the dough reaches the tops of the tins.

13 Ask an adult to preheat the oven to 350 degrees F (175 degrees C).

14 Bake the dough in a preheated oven for 45 to 50 minutes, or until bottom of the loaves sound hollow when tapped. Place on wire racks to cool.

What Happens

You have made bread! Heat from the oven made pockets of gas in the dough expand.

Why

- When flour is mixed into water and kneaded, proteins swell. These form gluten. Gluten can stretch and trap the bubbles of gas that make dough rise.
- The gas comes from the leavening (rising) action of yeast.
- Inside the dough, fermentation happens and molecules move.
- Enzymes from the yeast cells attack starch, and break it down into glucose.
- Other enzymes change the glucose molecules into carbon dioxide and ethanol. The carbon dioxide bubbles up through the mixture and makes the dough rise.

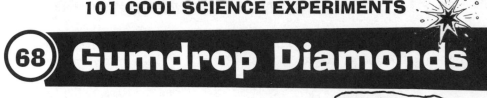

(68) Gumdrop Diamonds

Rat's Rating

Diamonds are so hard because of the shape of their structure. Why not build a model of a diamond structure that you can eat?

You will need:

gumdrops or marshmallows, toothpicks

Rat's Helpful Hint

Marshmallows are rather gooey. If you use them, your model will wobble. If you use gumdrops, you'll get a much stronger model.

What to do in this chemistry experiment

1 Push 3 toothpicks all the way into a gumdrop. They must be in a triangle shape so the gumdrop can stand.

2 Get another gumdrop and pick up another toothpick. Anchor the bottom legs together and start building upward.

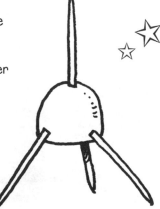

3 Keep building the shape. Every time toothpicks come together, anchor them with a gumdrop.

4 Start with a triangle-shaped base of 15 gumdrops with a gumdrop on each end of the toothpick.

5 Do you know what you have built?

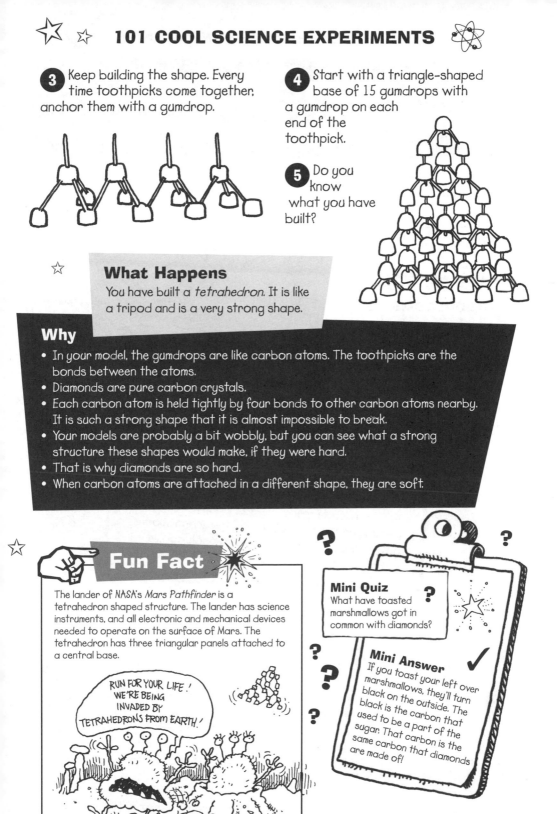

What Happens

You have built a *tetrahedron*. It is like a tripod and is a very strong shape.

Why

- In your model, the gumdrops are like carbon atoms. The toothpicks are the bonds between the atoms.
- Diamonds are pure carbon crystals.
- Each carbon atom is held tightly by four bonds to other carbon atoms nearby. It is such a strong shape that it is almost impossible to break.
- Your models are probably a bit wobbly, but you can see what a strong structure these shapes would make, if they were hard.
- That is why diamonds are so hard.
- When carbon atoms are attached in a different shape, they are soft.

Fun Fact

The lander of NASA's *Mars Pathfinder* is a tetrahedron shaped structure. The lander has science instruments, and all electronic and mechanical devices needed to operate on the surface of Mars. The tetrahedron has three triangular panels attached to a central base.

RUN FOR YOUR LIFE! WE'RE BEING INVADED BY TETRAHEDRONS FROM EARTH!

Mini Quiz
What have toasted marshmallows got in common with diamonds?

Mini Answer ✓
If you toast your left over marshmallows, they'll turn black on the outside. The black is the carbon that used to be a part of the sugar. That carbon is the same carbon that diamonds are made of!

69 # Want to Try a Hygroscopic Cookie?

Rat's Rating

Why do cookie manufactures package their products? Do this experiment and find out. You'll get to eat lots of cookies!

Would you care for one of my Home made Hygroscopic Cookies with your tea dear?

I don't mind if I do thanks Granny... But how do I stop at one?

You will need:

plain flour, sugar, honey, egg, baking powder, unsalted butter at room temperature, salt, lemon juice, flour sifter, egg beater, measuring cups, measuring spoons, 4 bowls (labeled A, B, C, D), wooden spoon, cookie sheet, parchment paper, oven mitt, PARENT SUPERVISION

What to do in this chemistry experiment

1 Get an adult to preheat the oven to 400 degrees Fahrenheit (200 degrees C).

2 Sift 1 cup of plain flour into bowl "A". Add 1/2 teaspoon baking powder and 1/2 teaspoon salt.

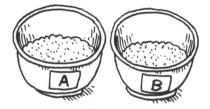

3 Sift 1 cup of plain flour into bowl "B". Add 1/2 teaspoon baking powder and 1/4 teaspoon salt.

4 Put 1/2 stick (2 oz/50 grams) of butter into bowl "C". Beat until creamy with eggbeater.

‖ Add 1/2 cup of sugar to the butter. Beat until mixed.

6 Beat the eggs. Tip half the egg into bowl "C".

 **7** Add the dry ingredients from Bowl "A". Add 2 tablespoons of water and 1/2 teaspoon lemon juice. Blend until smooth.

‖ In bowl "D", put 1/2 stick of soft butter. Add 1/4 cup honey. Beat until creamy.

 **9** Add the other half of the egg. Add the dry ingredients from bowl "B". Mix well.

10 Lay parchment paper on your cookie sheet, or grease the tray well.

11 Use a teaspoon to drop the batter from bowl "A" onto half of the cookie sheet.

12 Do the same with the batter from bowl "B". Keep a note of which cookies have sugar and which have honey.

13 Bake until brown around the edges. About 7 minutes.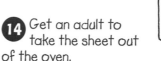

14 Get an adult to take the sheet out of the oven.

15 Let the cookies cool, then slide them onto a plate.

16 Eat a sugar cookie and a honey cookie. Are they the same crispness?

17 Leave both kinds of cookies out in the air. Take a bite every few hours. Which cookie loses its crispness more quickly?

What Happens
The honey cookie loses its crispness before the sugar cookie.

Why
- Cookies lose their crispness when they are left out in the air.
- It is the sweeteners in cookies that make this happen. This is because sweeteners absorb moisture.
- Sweeteners can make a cookie crisp or soft. Cookies made with sugars that are high in sucrose (granulated sugar and maple syrup) or glucose (corn syrup) stay crisp.
- Sweeteners high in fructose, such as honey, act differently. Fructose is hygroscopic (meaning it absorbs water from the air), so cookies made with a lot of honey get soft.

143

70 Smarty Pants

Rat's Rating

I might save the BLUE ones for the experiment ...no...I might eat those!

I'll save the RED ones... ...no..I like them too!

YELLOW? No..like them as well

OK! The experiment is off until further notice

Are colors just one color? Or are they a mixture of separate colors? Let's use candy to see how chromatography works.

You will need:
white coffee filter paper/white paper towels, bag of Smarties® or M&M's ® candy, water, plate, scissors

What to do in this physics experiment

1 Cut the paper filters into circles about 6 inches (15cm) across.

2 Place the plate on a flat surface. Lay the paper on the plate.

3 Place a candy in the center of the paper.

4 Dip your finger into the water. Hold it above the candy. Let enough water drip onto the candy so that the water starts going onto the paper.

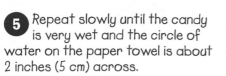

5 Repeat slowly until the candy is very wet and the circle of water on the paper towel is about 2 inches (5 cm) across.

6 Leave for a while, but keep checking. Something is going to happen.

WET PAPER TO HERE

What Happens

Rings of color form around the candy. Repeat with different colors – which color candy is made of the most different inks? Now, eat the candy! Once the shell is wet, what do you notice about the candy? It's not so crispy, is it?

Why

- The color in the sugarcoating of the candy shell dissolves in the water.
- The water is drawn out through the paper by capillary action. It moves in a growing circle.
- The different inks that make up the color of the candy move at different speeds and so they are separated.
- At the molecular level, smaller hydrophilic (a substance that loves water) molecules move faster through the paper.
- The colors that move the furthest from the candy have less of a mass than the ones closest to the candy.

Mini Quiz
Where did the idea for M&M's ® come from?

Mini Answer
The idea for M&M's ® came from the Spanish Civil War! The story is that on a trip to Spain, Forrest Mars Sr. met soldiers who were eating pellets of chocolate in a hard sugary coating. The coating stopped the chocolate from melting. Mr. Mars went back to his kitchen and invented the recipe for M&M's ®. They were first sold to the public in 1941 and were popular with American soldiers serving in World War II.

Fun Fact

We usually think of water running downhill, but capillary action makes water go up! Want to see how? Get a celery stalk. Put it in a jar with water and food coloring. The next day look at the celery. Cut the stalk and see how far up the stalk the colored water traveled. Try the same thing with a white flower such as a carnation, daisy, or chrysanthemum. How long does it take before the white petals change color?

Alfonse...I'm in one of those happy-go-lucky kind of moods. What color do you suggest?

I'd go for sticking you in a jar of 'VIVID ORANGE'

71 Iron for Breakfast

Feeling hungry? Would you eat an iron nail? Most enriched breakfast cereals add metallic iron as a health supplement. Try this experiment.

You will need:

2 different breakfast cereals (one healthy, one not!), bowls, pencil, magnets, ziplock plastic bags, tape, water, white coffee filters/paper towels, microscope or magnifying glass

What to do in this chemistry experiment

1 Put 1/2 cup of each cereal into 2 separate ziplock bags. Zip up the bags.

2 Use your hands to crush the cereal to a fine powder.

3 Pour each crushed cereal into a different bowl.

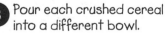

4 Add 1 cup of water to each bowl and stir. If needed, use extra water to keep the mixture thin and soupy.

6 Stir the cereal mix with the magnet for 10 minutes.

5 Tape a small magnet to the eraser end of a pencil. Seal it inside a plastic bag.

7 Lift out the magnet. What do you see? Gently wipe the magnet on the filter paper.

What Happens

Small bits of pure iron filings have collected on the magnet! The filings will look like small dark dots on the magnet. Sometimes they'll clump together. If you have trouble seeing the filings, try looking through a microscope or magnifying glass.

IRON FILINGS

Why
• Magnets attract iron.
• Magnets will stick to anything that has iron in it.
• Our bodies don't have very much iron, so magnets don't stick to us.

Fun Fact

The human body needs iron for many functions. Most importantly, iron is used to make *hemoglobin* in red blood cells. It is the iron in the hemoglobin that attracts oxygen molecules. This lets the blood cells carry oxygen to other cells in the body. Red blood cells are always being replaced. This is why your diet needs a constant supply of iron. Iron is put in some foods and vitamin pills as a healthy additive.

A little too much of that IRON enriched breakfast cereal

Mini Quiz
Is the iron in cereals the same iron as found in nails, cars, and machinery?

Mini Answer
Yes! The iron in cereal is pure iron! Really! It's mixed in the cereal batter along with other additives. The tiny particles of iron quickly react with hydrochloric acid and other chemicals in the digestive tract. This changes them into a form easily absorbed by the body.

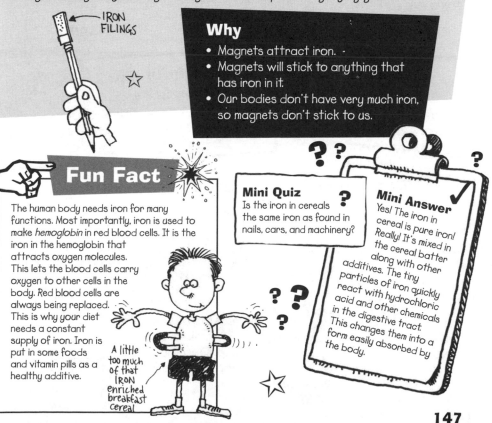

Under Pressure

(72) Will Humpty-Dumpty Crack Under Pressure?

Rat's Rating

Are eggshells fragile? Or do they have super strength? Try this egg-citing egg-speriment to find out.

Now we've got an egg cracking PRESSURE TEST coming up... So... have we got any HUMPTYs in here?

Not me ...I'm GREG

No...I'm BOB!

I'm STEWART!

I'm ROSEMARY!

You will need:
eggshell halves, cup, masking tape, fingernail scissors, canned food, piece of cardboard box

Rat's Helpful Hint
Don't ever use reptile eggs. They may hatch into young alligators, snakes or lizards. That would definitely spoil the experiment.

What to do in this forces experiment

1 Wrap a strip of masking tape around the middle of 4 eggshell halves. Keep a gap between the ends of the masking tape.

LEAVE A GAP HERE

2 Carefully, make a hole in the eggshell between the gap in the tape.

3 Empty the insides into a cup. Keep the empty eggshells.

4 Put the nail scissors into the hole.

5 Cut around the middle of the eggshell covered with the masking tape.

6 Separate the halves.

7 Trim off any jagged pieces of eggshell. Each one needs a straight-edged bottom.

8 Lay the eggshells, dome side up, so they make a square.

9 Place the piece of cardboard box on top.

10 Stand a can on top of the cardboard.

What Happens

Did the eggshells crack? Stack another can on top of the first one. Will the eggs crack now? Keep stacking the cans. How many cans are you able to stack before any of the eggs crack? Can you beat our record of 11 cans? How much weight did the eggs hold?

Why

- The strength of the egg is in its dome shape.
- No single point in the dome supports the whole weight of the cans on top of it.
- The weight spreads along the curved walls to the wide base. Allowing the eggshell to hold more weight.

Fun Fact

Can't remember if an egg is raw, or hard-boiled? Just spin the egg on its side and hold it for a moment. Let go. If the egg stops, it is hard-boiled. If it keeps spinning, the egg is raw. This is because a raw egg still has liquid inside. When you hold the egg, the liquid keeps turning. When you release the egg, the spinning liquid inside keeps the egg turning.

HARD BOILED EGGS stop spinning... RAW ones keep spinning... So what does it mean when it flies right off the table?

Mini Quiz

If all the eggs eaten in the world in one week were put end to end, how far do you think they would reach?

Mini Answer ✔

The line of eggs would reach from the earth to beyond the moon!

(73) The Invisible Shield

Rat's Rating

I wish this rain would stop so I could use my INVISIBLE SHIELD to deflect incoming missiles or bad guys...and not just rain.

Is air strong? Can it protect you? Air is all around you, but do you pay any attention to it? Can something you can't see, like air, protect something you can see, like a newspaper?

You will need:
newspaper, small empty glass, bowl of cold water, a rainy day (optional)

Rat's Helpful Hint
Don't use the newspaper before your Mom has read the sports page and Dad has cut out recipes from the Lifestyle section. Shredded newspaper from your pet's cage, or litter tray will not work!

What to do in this forces experiment

1 Stand in the rain. Put 1/2 a sheet of newspaper over your head. Does the paper stop you from getting wet? No, the water soaks into the paper, doesn't it?

2 Get another dry 1/2 sheet of newspaper.

3 Push the newspaper into the glass. It must be pushed in tightly. Make sure the newspaper is clear of the rim.

4 Turn the glass upside down.

5 Sink the glass into a bowl of water. The rim of the glass must rest on the bol lom of the bowl.

6 Hold the glass there. Count to 10.

7 Take the glass straight out of the water. Wipe the rim.

8 Turn the glass the right side up. Do you think the newspaper will be wet or dry?

9 Take out the newspaper and see.

What Happens
The newspaper is dry!

Crumply... but nice and dry!

Why
- Air molecules are invisible. But they still have weight, so they take up space.
- Water can't get into the glass because the glass is actually full of air molecules.
- When the glass is pushed into the water, the molecules don't escape. Instead, they are pressed together.
- The air can't get out because it is lighter than water. The air acts as a shield between the water and the newspaper. Some water may enter the glass, but not enough to wet the paper.

Fun Fact

Air pressure can tell us what kind of weather to expect. A high pressure system usually means clear skies. If a low pressure system is coming, then look for storms and rain.

A rather large LOW PRESSURE SYSTEM moved in between the bus stop and our front door catching me off guard dear!

Mini Quiz
Earth's atmosphere presses against every part of you. It does this with a force of 14.7 pounds per square inch (1 kg per square cm). Over a square foot (1,000 square cm) the force is almost one ton! What stops air pressure from squashing you?

Mini Answer
The air molecules inside your body stop you from being squashed. The air inside you balances the pressure outside. This keeps you firm and not squishy. The next time someone says that they are "under pressure" you'd better agree with them.

(74) Balloon Lung

Another Birthday Party! That means BALLOON LUNG!

What does your lung look like when it breathes air? Find out!

You will need:

clear plastic bottle,
balloon,
plastic funnel

Rat's Helpful Hint

Make sure the bottle has your favorite drink. That way you'll get a chance to drink it all before you start the experiment.

What to do in this anatomy experiment

1 Blow up and let out the air in a balloon 10 times. This makes it soft and baggy.

2 Push the balloon 1/2 inch (1cm) over the neck of a funnel about 5 inch (14 cm) wide.

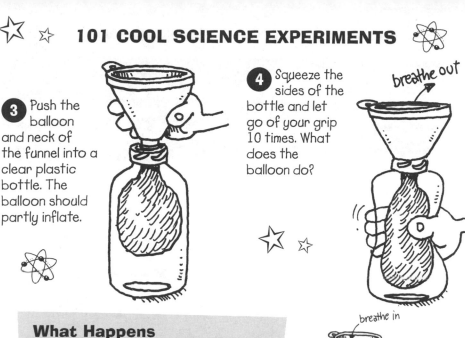

3 Push the balloon and neck of the funnel into a clear plastic bottle. The balloon should partly inflate.

4 Squeeze the sides of the bottle and let go of your grip 10 times. What does the balloon do?

breathe out

breathe in

What Happens

The balloon is breathing just like a real lung.

Why

- The air is forced out of the balloon.
- When you release your grip, the balloon fills again.
- When you breathe in, the muscles in your chest cavity contract and expand.
- This makes the pressure in the chest cavity lower than the outside air pressure.
- Air then flows in through the airways and inflates the lungs.
- When you breathe out, your muscles relax. Your chest cavity gets smaller.
- The decrease in volume of the cavity increases the pressure in the chest cavity above the outside air pressure.
- Air from the lungs (high pressure) then flows out of the airways to the outside air (low pressure). The cycle then repeats with each breath.

Fun Fact

Forests are the "lungs" of the world as we need them for the air we breathe. To survive, a tree uses carbon dioxide and gives off oxygen. They are like oxygen factories and are essential to the survival of the planet.

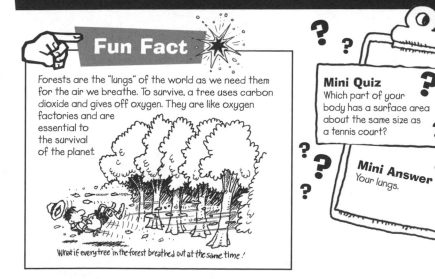

What if every tree in the forest breathed out at the same time!

Mini Quiz
Which part of your body has a surface area about the same size as a tennis court?

Mini Answer ✓
Your lungs.

75

Who Won?
It's a Straw

Rat's Rating

What's that? You need my STRAW for an experiment? Maybe come back later. I'm enjoying my Lemonade!

Do you think you can use a straw to pull liquid up into your mouth? No you can't! Find out why.

You will need:
drinking straw, drinking glasses, water

What to do in this forces experiment

1 Half fill one glass with water.

2 Put the straw in the glass.

3 Suck a small amount of water into the straw.

4 Hold your finger across the top of the straw. Take the straw out of the water.

5 Place the straw over the second empty glass.

6 Take your finger away from the top of the straw. Watch the water.

What Happens
The water comes out.

Why
- When you suck through a straw, you don't pull the liquid up. What you're doing is taking away some of the air inside the straw.
- This makes the pressure inside the straw lower than the pressure outside.
- The greater pressure of the outside air then pushes the water in the glass up through the straw and into your mouth.• When your finger covers the top of the straw, the water stays in the straw.
- It lessens the pressure of the air from above the straw.
- The greater air pressure under the straw holds the water inside it.

Fun Fact

In 1888, Marvin Stone patented the spiral winding process to make the first paper drinking straws. Before this, drinkers used natural rye grass straws. Stone made his original straw by winding strips of paper around a pencil and gluing it together. He then used paraffin coated manila paper, so the straws wouldn't become soggy while someone was drinking. In 1906, Stone's company invented a machine to wind the straws.

I hope one day someone invents the perfect drinking straw... one made out of plastic! I've never been much for the taste of bamboo.

Mini Quiz
Can you keep water upside down in a glass?

Mini Answer ✓
Yes, you can! Fill a drinking glass completely with water. Cover the top of the glass with a piece of heavy paper. Hold it down so the card touches the rim all the way around. Turn the glass upside down and carefully remove your hand. The water stays in the glass!

76 I can. Can You?

Rat's Rating

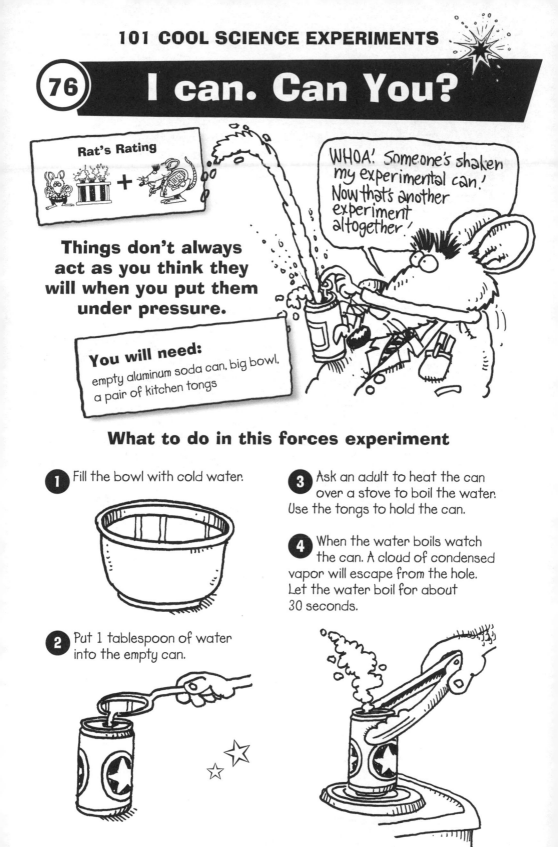

Things don't always act as you think they will when you put them under pressure.

WHOA! Someone's shaken my experimental can! Now that's another experiment altogether!

You will need:
empty aluminum soda can, big bowl, a pair of kitchen tongs

What to do in this forces experiment

1 Fill the bowl with cold water.

3 Ask an adult to heat the can over a stove to boil the water. Use the tongs to hold the can.

4 When the water boils watch the can. A cloud of condensed vapor will escape from the hole. Let the water boil for about 30 seconds.

2 Put 1 tablespoon of water into the empty can.

5 Quickly turn the can upside down and dip it into the water in the bowl. Does the water in the bowl flow into the hole in the can? Or does something else happen?

What Happens

Bang! The can will collapse almost immediately. Some water from the pan may get into the can, but not fast enough to fill the can before the air outside crushes it.

BANG!

Why

- When you heat the can you make the water boil.
- The vapor from the boiling water pushes the cool air out of the can.
- When the can is filled with water vapor, it is cooled suddenly when turned upside down in the water.
- Cooling the can condenses the water vapor inside the can.
- This leaves less air in the can than there was originally. When this happens, the pressure of the air outside the can is greater than the pressure inside. This causes the air outside to crush the can.

Fun Fact

You can crush an open aluminum can with your hand. When you squeeze on the can, the pressure outside becomes greater than the pressure inside. If you squeeze hard enough, the can collapses.

I think the idea is to drink what's in the can before you crush it.

CRUNCH

Mini Quiz
How long does it take an aluminum can to decompose?

Mini Answer
It takes over 500 years for an aluminum can to decompose.

It's a Pushover

Magical Marbles

Rat's Rating

I would have been the wizard of the rat hole as a kid if I'd had these!

ABRACADABRA

MAGIC MARBLES

**Inertia is the way a body will stay still,
or move, unless acted upon by an external force.
Want to see how it works?
You'll have to move your body then!**

You will need:
2 rulers, marbles, tape

What to do in this physics experiment

1 Tape the rulers to a flat surface. They need to be parallel and about 1/2 inch (1.5 cm) apart.

2 Put 2 marbles in the middle of the rulers a few inches (5 cm) apart

3 Gently tap 1 marble so it rolls and hits the second one. What happens?

What Happens

The marble that had been rolling stops. And the one that had been still, now rolls! The force of the rolling marble transfers to the other one. It stops the first and sets the second in motion. Now put two marbles on the stick so they touch and a third marble several inches (cm) away. Gently tap the single marble into the other two. Notice that the rolling marble stops, the middle one stays still and the third one rolls! The momentum went through the second marble into the third! Try other combinations, two marbles into three still marbles, or three into three. You will find that however many marbles you set in motion, the same number will be made to roll when they are hit.

This one keeps going

This one stops

Why

- Inertia is the way one object sets another object in motion.
- An object at rest tends to stay at rest. An object that is moving tends to keep moving in the same direction.
- An object stays at rest, or keeps moving, unless some external force acts upon it.

Fun Fact

Can a paper straw go through a raw potato? Here is another inertia activity. Put a potato on the kitchen counter. If the potato is old, soak it in water for 30 minutes first. Hold it firmly with one hand. Make sure your hand is not underneath the potato. With a fast, strong push, stab the potato with the straw. The straw pierces the potato without bending, or buckling.

People go to all the trouble to get a straw into a potato.... But then what are you supposed to do with it?

Suck out the juice?

Mini Quiz How can something as soft as a stalk of grain go through a wall?

Mini Answer ✓ Inertia causes stalks in fields to go into and through wooden barns and houses when propelled by tornado force winds at least 110mph (177 km/h).

78 Get a Move On

Rat's Rating

WHOA!
Who greased the slide..?

Do some objects move more easily than others?

You will need:
matchbox, stone, small wooden block, eraser, flat-sided glass bottle, ice cube or a selection of similar objects, chopping board or smooth piece of wood, metal tray

Rat's Helpful Hint
On a school day, if you move out of bed more slowly than others do, just blame it on friction!

What to do in this friction experiment

1 Put your objects in a line at one end of the chopping board.

2 Slowly lift this end of the board until the objects begin to move. What objects move first?

3 Repeat the experiment, but put your objects on a metal tray. Do the objects move more easily?

What Happens

Some of your objects will move more easily than others. Feel the ones that move easily. They will feel smooth. Anything rough will not move as easily.

Why

- Each surface has a different amount of friction with the surface of the board.
- Anything smooth will slide down first. The smooth sides move easily over the board.
- Rough items make more friction. They will slide more slowly.
- Any rubbery surface will hardly move because it makes strong friction.

Fun Fact

Friction also makes it hard for objects to move in water. Get a smooth rubber ball and a tennis ball. Put a small amount of water in a shallow bowl. Put a ball in each bowl. Spin each ball. Which one moves more easily? The smooth surface makes less friction so the rubber ball moves more easily than the tennis ball. This is why a fast boat has a smooth hull.

Mini Quiz
How can friction help a falling cat?

Mini Answer ✓
A cat knows about friction! It knows that increasing its mass leads to more friction or air resistance. When a cat falls, it rights itself. It spreads its legs to make a sort of cat parachute! The rising air has a bigger area to push against. This slows the cat's fall and allows it to land on its feet. But don't try this on your poor kitty.

(79) Am I Attractive?

Rat's Rating

OK! I'm lost! I'm a SCIENTIST not an explorer!

Magnets are more human than you think. Their poles can attract each other as well as repel each other.

You will need: ☆
modeling clay, sharp pencil with an eraser, horseshoe magnet

Rat's Helpful Hint
Just remember to keep your magnet away from audio and videotapes and computer disks, or you might erase the information on them!

What to do in this magnets experiment

1 Roll the piece of clay into a ball.

2 Flatten it to make a cone shape.

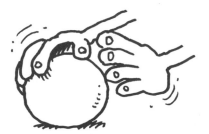

3 Push the eraser end of the pencil into the clay.

4 Carefully balance the horseshoe magnet on the pencil lead.

What Happens
The magnet slowly moves itself into a north-south direction.

NORTH – SOUTH

Why
- The Earth has a magnetic field, which isn't very strong, but it's enough to attract your magnet. The magnet turned in a north/south direction.
- Five billion years ago the Earth was made in a big mix of meteorites and comets. The huge amount of heat melted the planet. It's still cooling off today!
- Denser materials like iron from the meteorites sank to create the core of the Earth. As it rotated, it made a magnetic field.

Fun Fact

Cows like to graze on grass. Unfortunately, bolts, nails, and bits of barbed wire end up in the grass. The cows eat these by mistake. Some cows have even died when trying to pass them through their digestive system. To solve the problem, farmers can feed calves magnets! The magnets stay in the cow's stomachs their whole life and hold onto the metal. This means the metal doesn't go through their digestive systems.

Mini Quiz
Imagine that you are in the middle of the ocean. All you see is water and it is a cloudy day so you cannot see the sun. How would you know which way to go?

Mini Answer ✓
No matter where you are on earth, you can hold a compass and it will point toward the North Pole. Long before space satellites and other high-tech navigational aids, a compass was the best way to know which way to go.

She calls it.. 'a magnetic personality'. But I think there's something else going on there!

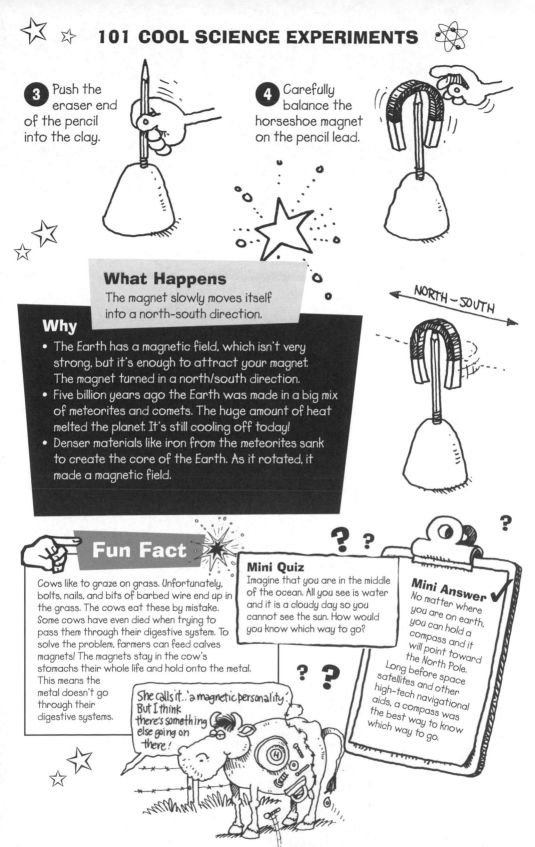

Do s This Mak Sense?

You Smell!

Rat's Rating

I can smell.... A RAT!

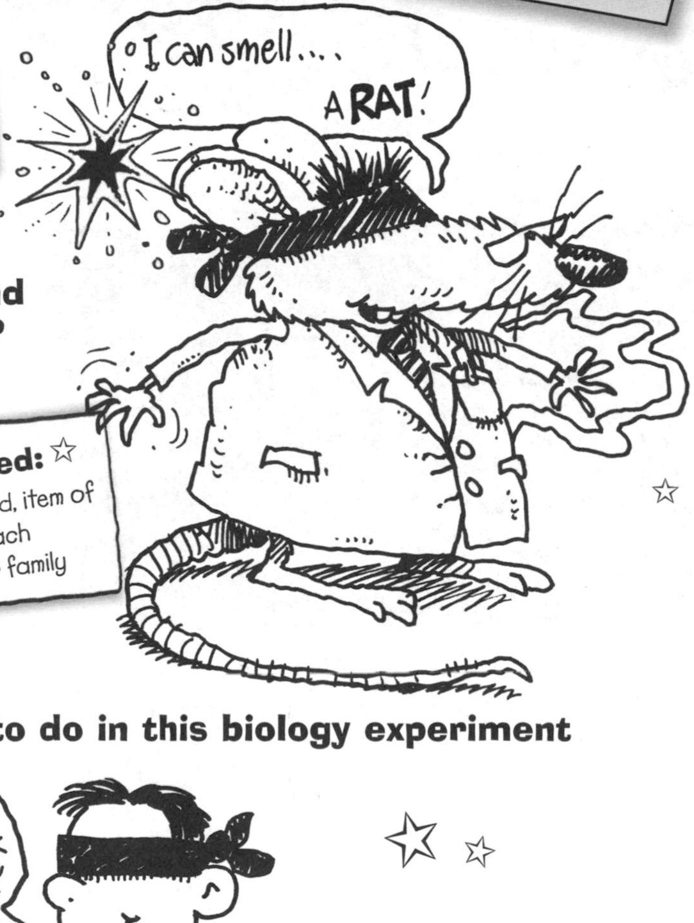

Want to find out more?

You will need: ☆
a friend, blindfold, item of clothing from each member of your family

What to do in this biology experiment

Boy! It's black in here!

1 Put on the blindfold. Don't peek.

2 Ask your friend to get an item of clothing that someone has just taken off. Hopefully, not smelly socks! Have something from each member of your family.

3 Get your friend to hold the clothing under your nose. But don't touch it.

4 Concentrate and tell whose clothing it is just by the smell.

Remember the time when the mouse crawled under the refrigerator and died? Well this smells like that!

What Happens
You should be able to tell which item of clothing belongs to each family member.

Why
- The smell comes from the *pheromones* our body makes.
- We all have own special smell. The smell is ours alone and different from anyone else.
- We get used to these smells and don't notice them.
- Our smells even change the fragrance of perfume or cologne. That's why these are a little different on every person. It's also the reason different houses smell differently.

Fun Fact

Be careful not to squash a yellowjacket wasp near its nest. A dying yellowjacket gives out an alarm pheromone. This calls other wasps to come and help. Within 15 seconds, yellowjackets within a 15 foot (4.5 meter) area will attack you for squashing their friend!

IT WAS AN ACCIDENT!! I DIDN'T MEAN TO SQUASH YOUR FRIEND!

He had dark hair... medium build... with big boots... and he went that-a-way!

Mini Quiz Why do feet often smell so bad?

Mini Answer ✓
Very tiny plants and animals grow on your skin and inside you. Gross! But true!

These microbes make your feet smell bad, because as they grow they're smelly. We can wash some of them off, but microbes duplicate, so we can never get rid of them completely. When something is clean of all microbes, it's sterile. But microbes always get back in eventually. We are protected from most of the bad ones by our body's immune system.

81 Eye Don't Believe It!

Rat's Rating

WHOA.' No head! Well either... The mirror is on the blink... I've lost my head... Or it's something to do with the next experiment...'

Hope it comes back.'

Usually both eyes receive much the same view of things. You blend these Views into a single three-dimensional picture.

What happens when your eyes receive different images?

You will need:
chairs, hand-held mirror approximately 4 to 6 inches (10 to 15 cm) on a side, white wall or white surface (white poster board works well), a friend

What to do in this biology experiment

1 Sit on a chair. Have a white wall on your right.

2 Have a friend sit very still on a chair a few feet (meters) away. They need to be against a plain, light-colored background.

3 Hold the bottom of the mirror with your left hand. Put the mirror edge against your nose. You want the reflecting surface of the mirror to face sideways, toward the white surface.

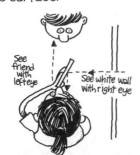

See friend with left eye

See white wall with right eye

4 Keep the mirror edge against your nose and stay very still. Rotate the mirror so that your right eye sees just the reflection of the white wall. And your left eye looks forward at the face of your friend. Focus on just one feature of their face.

5 Move your hand very slowly in front of the white surface as if wiping a window clean. What don't you see?

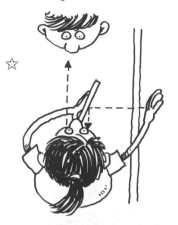

What Happens

Parts of your friend's face disappear! If this doesn't work, one of your eyes might be stronger than the other. Try the experiment again, but this time switch the eye you use to look at the person and the eye you use to look at the wall. People vary greatly in their ability to see this effect. You may have to try this several times. Give yourself time to see the effect and don't give up too soon!

It might look as though my eyes have completely disappeared

But I can still see you!

Why

- Your two eyes usually see very slightly different pictures of the world around you.
- Your brain analyzes these two pictures. It then combines them to make a single, three-dimensional image.
- The mirror lets your eyes see two very different views.
- One eye looks straight ahead at your friend. The other eye looks at the white wall and your moving hand.
- Your brain tries to put together a picture that makes sense by selecting bits and pieces from both views.
- Your brain is very sensitive to changes and movement. Since your friend is sitting so still, your brain highlights the information coming from the moving hand, and parts of the face disappear.
- No one knows how or why parts of the face sometimes stay, but the eyes and the mouth seem to be the last features to disappear.

Fun Fact

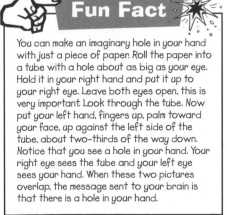

You can make an imaginary hole in your hand with just a piece of paper. Roll the paper into a tube with a hole about as big as your eye. Hold it in your right hand and put it up to your right eye. Leave both eyes open, this is very important. Look through the tube. Now put your left hand, fingers up, palm toward your face, up against the left side of the tube, about two-thirds of the way down. Notice that you see a hole in your hand. Your right eye sees the tube and your left eye sees your hand. When these two pictures overlap, the message sent to your brain is that there is a hole in your hand.

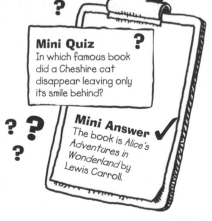

Mini Quiz
In which famous book did a Cheshire cat disappear leaving only its smile behind?

Mini Answer ✓
The book is *Alice's Adventures in Wonderland* by Lewis Carroll.

(82) Are You a Super Taster?

Rat's Rating

Everything tastes great to me! I'm a RAT... I eat anything!

How many times have you heard, "No dessert until you eat all your veggies"? Sometimes you have to decide which is better, skipping your veggies or getting dessert. Well, taste is an important sense. Let's see how good yours is.

You will need:
dark food coloring, cotton ball, piece of white paper, hole punch (the standard size used for a three-ring binder), mirror

What to do in this anatomy experiment

1 Use the hole punch to make a small hole in a piece of paper.

2 Take the cotton ball and dip it into the food coloring.

3 Wipe the color across the tip of your tongue.

4 Put the colored part of your tongue through the hole in the paper.

5 Look in the mirror.

6 Count the round bumps on your tongue that appear in the paper hole.

Count the bumps you see here

What Happens

If you have 25 or more round bumps on your tongue, you are a super taster! If you have less than 25, you are an ordinary taster. Some people have such sensitive and refined taste buds that they find some nice tasting foods gross. The taste buds are mainly found on or between bumps called *papillae*. Papillae cover the tongue surface and you can see them with the naked eye.

Why

- Your tongue has four basic types of taste buds: bitter, sour, salty, and sweet.
- The more taste buds you have the better your sense of taste.
- You have about 10,000 taste buds on your tongue! Each of these is made up of between 50 - 150 receptor cells.
- Taste buds live for only 1 to 2 weeks before being replaced by new ones.
- Each receptor in a taste bud responds best to one of the four basic tastes. A receptor can respond to the other three tastes, but it responds strongest to a particular taste.
- You also have a few taste buds on the lips (especially salt-sensitive ones), the inside of the cheeks, under your tongue, the roof of your mouth and the back of your throat.

Fun Fact

When you eat very hot food or drink very hot drinks you burn your tongue. When this happens, you burn off your taste buds too! To make sure you never lose your sense of taste, your taste buds flip over. They rebuild themselves while a new set goes to work.

I DO IT ALL FOR SCIENCE

Brace yourselves guys! Here comes another jug of steaming hot coffee!

Mini Quiz ❓
Do insects have taste buds?

Mini Answer
Most insects use their mouths to taste flavors just as you do. Some insects use other parts of their bodies to taste with, too! A butterfly tastes food with its mouth and its feet. An ant can taste food with its mouth and with its antennae.

Jelly Belly

83

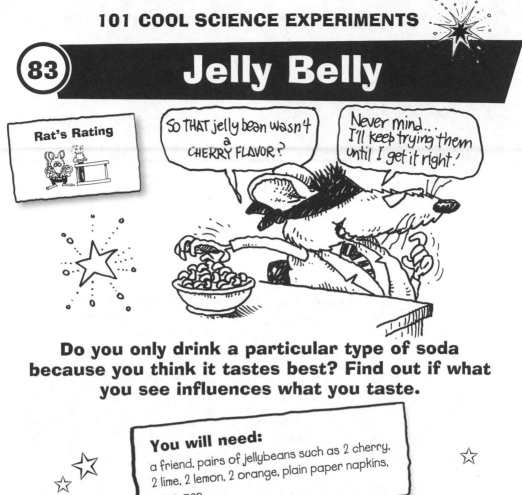

Rat's Rating

SO THAT jelly bean wasn't a CHERRY FLAVOR?

Never mind... I'll keep trying them until I get it right!

Do you only drink a particular type of soda because you think it tastes best? Find out if what you see influences what you taste.

You will need:
a friend, pairs of jellybeans such as 2 cherry, 2 lime, 2 lemon, 2 orange, plain paper napkins, cups, pen

What to do in this biology experiment

1 Divide the jellybeans into two groups. Each group should have one of each flavor.

2 Label small napkins with the numbers 1–4.

3 Place the jellybeans from Group A on a napkin – one jellybean on each napkin.

4 Put the jellybeans from Group B into 4 cups so that your friend can't see them.

5 Label these cups with the numbers 1–4. Make sure that the flavors of Group B have different numbers than the flavors from Group A.

6 Tell your friend the names of the flavors they'll be testing.

7 Get your friend to look at the jellybean on napkin number 1 from Group A and then taste the jelly bean and write down its flavor. Do the same thing with jellybeans numbered 2 – 4 on the napkins.

8 Keep the color of the jellybeans in Group B hidden. Get your friend to close his or her eyes and taste the jellybeans. Write down the flavors that your friend says each jellybean tastes like. You can even say that the flavors are the same as before. How many did your friend get right?

What Happens

When you don't see the color of the jellybean, you often give the wrong answer.

That last one was definitely LEMON!

SORRY! ORANGE!

Why

- The senses of sight and taste are technically not related. But they can have a strong mental influence on each other.
- Your friend couldn't see the colors of the jellybeans. Jellybeans don't have a strong smell either. Taste was the only sense left.
- Your taste bud cells have a pit of a very definite shape. When a substance with the matching chemical shape comes along, the receptor cell sends a signal to the brain. This gives the brain clues as to what you are eating.

Fun Fact

Half fill 2 drinking glasses with 2 different flavored and different colored sodas – orange, grape, cherry etc. Half fill another glass with 1 unflavored clear soda (like fizzy mineral water). Add food coloring to the clear soda. You need a color to match the color of one of the flavored sodas. This will make it look like a flavored soda, but of course, it won't have any taste.
Get a friend to tell you what each drink tastes like. Chances are they said their unflavored drink was a flavor that matched the color.

It doesn't taste like anything... I just drink it for the COLOR!

Mini Quiz
Is eyesight important when we eat?

Mini Answer ✓
In sighted people, eyes are the first sense that decides whether something looks good enough to eat. Colors are very important. Would you eat a blue burger? Food companies add color to food to make it look better, although the taste stays the same. People like to see foods in colors that they expect. Butter is a pale yellow. But people think butter should be bright yellow, so some manufacturers add yellow color to the butter.

84 You've Got a Nerve

Rat's Rating

AAARRR! That hit a nerve!!

How sensitive are you? Try this and see.

You will need:
color pencils, bobby pins, piece of card, compass, scissors, ruler, a friend

What to do in this anatomy experiment

1 With the ruler mark off 1, 2 and 3 inches (or 3, 6, 9 cm) markings on the card.

2 Use the compass to draw a circle at each of the three markings. You now have 3 zones – inner, outer, and center.

3 Cut around the outside of the large circle.

4 Color in the 3 zones in three separate colors.

5 Ask your friend to shut his/her eyes.

6 Stick some bobby pins in the center zone. Keep the bobby pins at the same height.

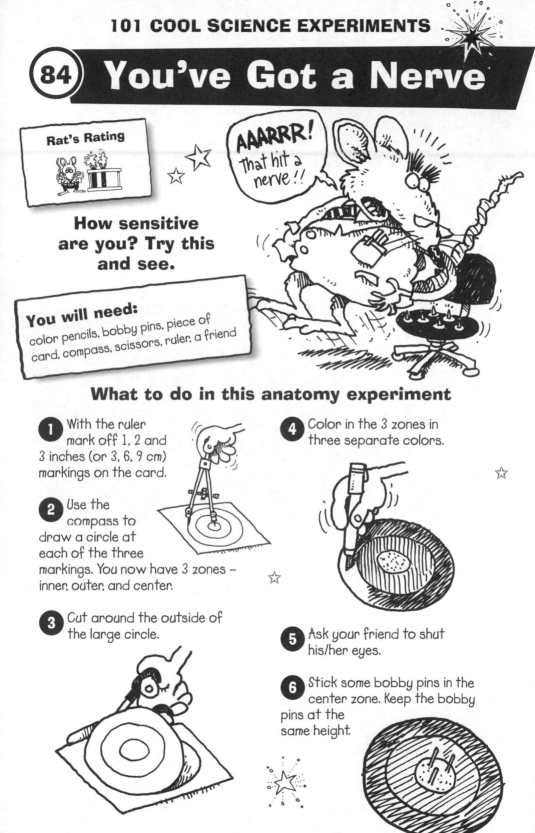

7 Press the bobby pins firmly against the arm of your friend. Ask your friend how many bobby pins are felt.

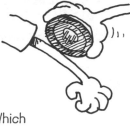

8 Repeat with the bobby pins stuck in the inner and outer zones.

9 Test the skin on the palm, fingers, and thumb tips. Which part of your friend's skin is the most sensitive?

Why
- Your body is full of nerve endings. These are in your skin and different tissues.
- Parts of your body, including the arm don't have many nerve endings. It makes it hard for these parts to feel the separate pressures from the bobby pins.
- Your fingers and thumb tips have an extra number of nerve endings. This makes it much easier for you to get accurate results. This is why you feel more pain in areas with more nerve endings.

What Happens
The arm is not very sensitive. You can only tell how many bobby pins are in the outer zone. Your palm is less sensitive. You can feel each bobby pin in the inner zone, but not in the center zone. Your fingertips are very sensitive. You can feel each one of the bobby pins in the center zone.

Fun Fact
Most people are ticklish on the bottom of their feet. This is because your feet have such large nerve endings and these make them very sensitive. That is also why a tiny stone in your shoe feels like a rock!

Now I know a rock in my shoe when I feel one... And I feel one now!

Mini Quiz
Pain relief medicine can stop pain. But how does the medicine know the location of the pain?

Mini Answer
When you take medicine to stop pain, it doesn't go straight to the pain. It only seems that way, because the pain goes away from the exact spot that hurts! Actually, the pain reliever works with your cells, your nerve endings, your nervous system, and your brain to stop you feeling the pain. Some nerve endings can sense pain. When cells in your body are hurt, they let out a chemical. The special nerve endings that sense pain are very sensitive to this chemical. When it is let out the nerve endings respond. They pick up and send the pain and injury messages through the nervous system to the brain. They tell the brain about the pain, like where it is and how much it hurts. The brain then responds – ouch!

85 Ghost Fish

Remember your Goldfish you threw in the bin after it died?

I'm the ghost of those fishfingers you had last week!

I was the Crumbed Sea Perch with the minimum of chips!

There's definitely something fishy going on here... Maybe it was that battered fish I had for dinner!

You see colors when receptor cells on the retina of your eye are stimulated by light. What happens if your eyes become tired?

You will need:
white pieces of card or paper, color paper – bright red, green and blue, black marker, scissors, glue

What to do in this anatomy experiment

1 Draw the same simple fish shape on each of the 3 colored papers. Cut out the shape.

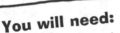

2 Glue each shape onto its own white card. Leave one white card blank.

BLANK CARD

3 Draw a small black eye with the marker for each fish. On the last white card, draw the outline of bowl for your fish.

4 Put the cards in a very bright area (it won't work if you don't!) Stare at the eye of the red fish for 15 to 20 seconds. Then quickly stare at the outline of the bowl. What do you see?

5 Now stare at the eye of the green fish for 15 to 20 seconds. Then quickly stare at the outline of the bowl. What do you see?

6 Finally, do the same with the blue fish. What do you see?

What Happens

Ghostly fish appear! The red fish is now in the bowl. But its color has changed to blue-green. The green fish is now in the bowl. But its color is now red-blue. The blue fish is now in the bowl. And its color has changed to yellow.

Why

- The ghostly fish that you see are *afterimages*.
- An afterimage is an image that stays with you even after you have stopped looking at the object.
- The back of your eye is lined with light-sensitive cells called *rods* and *cones*.
- Cones are sensitive to colored light. Each of the three types of cones is sensitive to a range of colors.
- When you stare at the red fish, the image falls on one area of your retina.
- The red-sensitive cells in that area grow tired. They stop responding strongly to red light.
- The white card reflects red, blue, and green light to your eyes. This is because white light is made up of all these colors.
- When you suddenly shift your gaze to the blank white card, the tired red-sensitive cells do not respond to the reflected red light. But the blue-sensitive and green-sensitive cones respond strongly to the reflected blue and green light.
- So, where the red-sensitive cells do not respond you see a bluish-green fish.
- When you stare at the green fish, your green-sensitive cones become tired.
- When you look at the white card, your eyes respond only to the reflected red and blue light, and you see a red-blue fish.
- When you stare at your blue fish, the blue-sensitive cones become tired and your eyes only respond to the reflected red and green light so you see a yellow fish.

Blind Test

86

Rat's Rating

CLUNK.

Who put that wall there? Oh.. it's part of the blind test!

If you were blind, how quickly would you learn to feel your way around? Would it be easier to do some things more than others? Here are some tests to help you find out.

You will need:
sheet of paper, sheet of lined paper, pencil

What to do in this biology experiment

1 Place a sheet of paper on a table. Make a circle about 1/2 inch (1.5 cm) around on the paper.

2 Lift your pencil high above your head. Shut your eyes. Lower your arm and make a dot on the paper as close as you can to the center of the circle. How close did you get to the center of the circle? Try again. How many times does it take before you get your dot inside the circle? Now try with your eyes open.

3 On a sheet of lined paper, sign your name.

4 Place your pencil after the signature on the same line. Shut your eyes, and sign your name again. Try writing other words. Can you tell the difference between what you wrote with your eyes closed and what you wrote with your eyes open?

What Happens

You'll make your dot outside the circle at first. It takes several tries before getting inside the circle. With writing your signature there is very little, if any, difference.

Why

- Most people find that looking at the circle between tests makes them do better.
- Your eyesight is very important for real accuracy.
- However, sight is not necessary for copying written words. You are used to the "feel" of writing from the nerves in your hands and fingers.

Fun Fact

A blind chameleon still changes colors. This is because chameleons don't change colors to match their background. Instead, their color changes are responses to light intensity, temperature, or how they are feeling.

Boy! That's a happy looking chameleon! What must it be thinking?

Mini Quiz How do people who can't see read?

Mini Answer People who can't see use Braille. Braille is a pattern of raised dots. The six dot positions are set out within a rectangular cell. Each cell is made by two side-by-side rows, each with three dots. Letters, numbers, sounds, and common words are shown by the pattern of dots in each cell.

87

What's Hot?
What's Not?

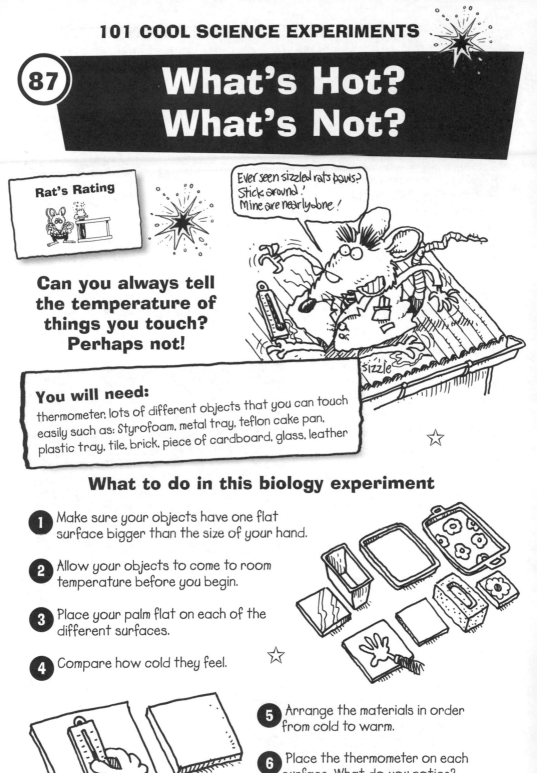

Rat's Rating

Ever seen sizzled rats paws? Stick around! Mine are nearly done!

Can you always tell the temperature of things you touch? Perhaps not!

You will need:
thermometer, lots of different objects that you can touch easily such as: Styrofoam, metal tray, teflon cake pan, plastic tray, tile, brick, piece of cardboard, glass, leather

What to do in this biology experiment

1 Make sure your objects have one flat surface bigger than the size of your hand.

2 Allow your objects to come to room temperature before you begin.

3 Place your palm flat on each of the different surfaces.

4 Compare how cold they feel.

5 Arrange the materials in order from cold to warm.

6 Place the thermometer on each surface. What do you notice?

What Happens

All the materials are at the same temperature! Your hand isn't always a good thermometer. When you touch a variety of objects, some will seem warmer or colder than others, even when they are at the same temperature.

Why

- The nerve endings in your skin are sensitive to temperature.
- They can tell the difference between your inside body temperature and your outside skin temperature.
- When your skin cools, these nerves tell you that the object you're touching is cold.
- An object that feels cold must be colder than your hand. It must carry your body heat away so that your skin cools down.
- Styrofoam and metal are two materials that work well for this experiment. They both start at room temperature and are both colder than your hand.
- They don't feel equally cold because they carry heat away from your hand at different rates.
- Styrofoam is an insulator. This means it is a very poor conductor of heat. When your hand touches the Styrofoam, heat flows from your hand to the Styrofoam and warms its surface. Because this heat is not conducted away quickly, the surface of the Styrofoam becomes as warm as your hand. This means little or no extra heat leaves your hand. There is no difference in temperature between the inside of your body and the outside of your skin. Your nerves sense no difference in temperature. The Styrofoam feels warm.
- Metal carries heat away quickly. Metal is a good conductor of heat. Heat flows from your hand into the metal. It is then conducted quickly away into the bulk of the metal.
- This leaves the metal surface and your skin surface cool. That is why metal feels cool.

Fun Fact

Your skin keeps a constant body temperature of 98.6 degrees Fahrenheit (37 degrees Celsius). When you feel neither hot or cold, you're not aware of the temperature. Keeping you at the right temperature depends on your skin being able to sense a temperature change.

That's why you can swim in cold water, yet have a hot bath.

Well your bath is too hot for me! I'm getting out!

Metoo! It's warping my hull!

Mini Quiz
How cold do animals get when they hibernate?

Mini Answer ✓
The body temperature of animals in hibernation plunges to just a few degrees above freezing. If they are disturbed they can die because it throws their bodies into shock.

Adventures with Air

88

Candle in the Wind

Rat's Rating

What is the connection between a candle experiment and the shape of a bird and airplane wing? Find out.

You will need:

a candle, low candle holder, cylinder-shaped container the same height as the candle – a metal or ceramic salt shaker is perfect, ADULT SUPERVISION

What to do in this forces experiment

1. Ask an adult to light a candle. Put it in a low holder and place it on the table.

2. Stand a salt container 3 inches (8 cm) in front of the candle.

3 Stand on the opposite side of the lit candle. Blow against the container. Make sure you keep your mouth even with the flame of the candle. Do you think you can blow out the candle? Of course not! The container's in the way. Or is it?

What Happens
The candle goes out!

Why
- Air follows the curved shape of the container.
- When the streams of air meet on the other side, they join to blow out the candle.

Fun Fact

You can make your own aerofoil. You'll need a piece of thin cardboard 6 in. x 9 in. (16 cm x 23 cm), tape, a pen, a drinking straw 2 in. (5 cm) long, and a piece of string 39 in. (100 cm). Fold the card in two leaving an overlap of 1/3 inch (1 cm). Push the overlapping ends together. This makes one side of the folded paper curve. Tape the ends together. Use a pen to make a hole through the middle of the wing. Carefully push a drinking straw through the hole. Thread the string through the straw. Pull the two ends of the string tight, holding one in each hand. Check the wing has the curved surface upwards and the wider surface is facing forwards. Keep holding the string tightly. Quickly run forward. Your aerofoil will move up the string.

Mini Quiz
Why are airplane wings and birds' wings curved?

Mini Answer
Airplane wings and the wings of birds are a special shape. In airplanes, this shape is known as an aerofoil. As they move forward, air is forced over and under the wing. The wings curve so the top edge has a larger surface than underneath. Both the upper and lower surfaces of the wing deflect air. The upper surface of the wing deflects air downward because the airflow "sticks" to the wing surface and follows the angle of the wing. This difference in pressure between the top and bottom of the wing results in an upward force, or lift, on the wing.

89 Friendly Apples

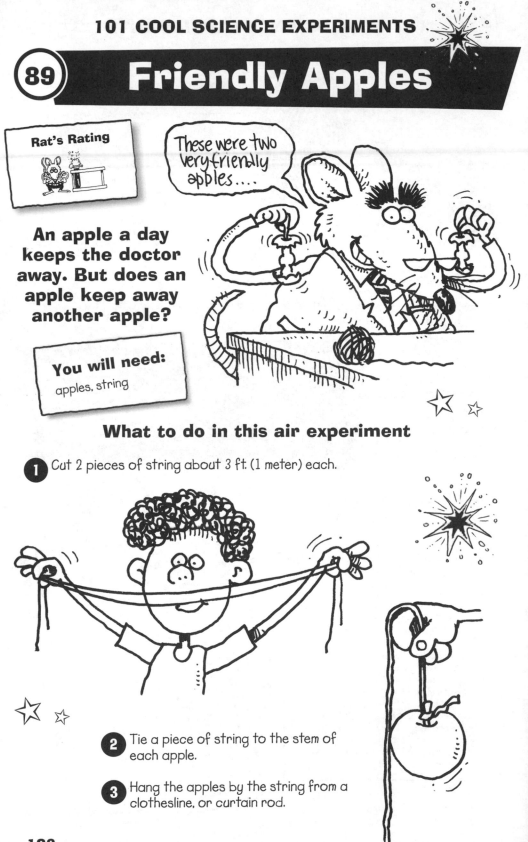

Rat's Rating

These were two very friendly apples....

An apple a day keeps the doctor away. But does an apple keep away another apple?

You will need:
apples, string

What to do in this air experiment

1 Cut 2 pieces of string about 3 ft. (1 meter) each.

2 Tie a piece of string to the stem of each apple.

3 Hang the apples by the string from a clothesline, or curtain rod.

4 Hold the apples two inches (5 cm) apart. What do you think will happen if you blow between the apples? Will they move further apart, pushed by the stream of air? Of course, you think!

5 Blow very hard between the apples.

What Happens
The apples come together!

Why
- As the speed of the air gets faster, the pressure of the air gets less.
- When you blow, the air between the apples moves. This means that the air pressure there is less than on the other sides of the apples where the air is still.
- The air on the side of the apples pushes them towards the area of lower pressure and the apples come together.

Fun Fact

Lay a bottle with a small mouth on a table. Roll a wad of paper into a pea-sized ball. Put the paper into the mouth of the bottle. Blow hard and fast. Instead of flying into the bottle, the paper flies out at you! Fast moving air goes past the paper and hits the bottom of the bottle. This increases the air pressure inside the bottle. As the compressed air rushes out, it carries the paper with it.

BINK!

Mini Quiz ?
How can a straw work like a bug spray?

Mini Answer ✓
Half fill a glass of water. Stand a plastic straw upright in the glass. The water will reach as high in the straw as it does in the glass. Hold another straw close to the top of the first straw. Put it at a right angle to the top end of the first straw and blow through it. Watch the water level rise. The fast flowing stream of air makes a decrease in air pressure. Blow very hard. The water rises to the opening and sprays out. You've now atomized the water into fine droplets. Cleaning sprays, insect sprays, and perfume atomizers work in the same way.

90 Floating Ball

Rat's Rating

A rat needs to have his fur looking just right for the big match!

That includes eye brows!

Can a ball float on an invisible stream of air?

You will need:
a hair dryer, ping-pong ball/round balloon/Styrofoam ball, tissue

What to do in this physics experiment

1 Turn on the hair dryer.

2 Blow a stream of air straight up.

3 Carefully balance the ping-pong ball above the stream of air.

4 Pull it slowly out of the stream. What do you see? When only half the ball is out of the stream of air, you can feel it being sucked back.

5 Let go of the ball. It will waver back and forth and then settle near the center of the stream of air.

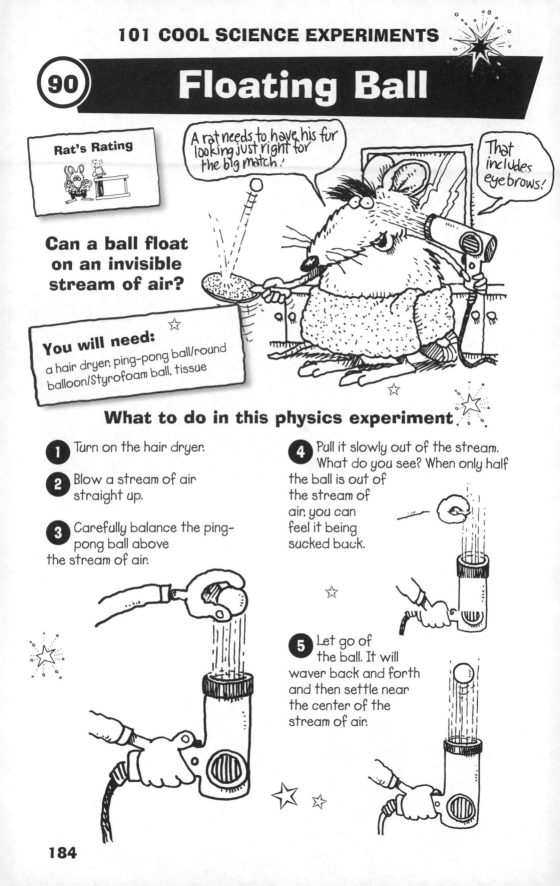

6 Keep the ball a little way out of the stream of air. With the other hand, dangle a tissue and look for the stream of air above the ball. See how the ball turns the stream outward.

☆

7 Tilt the stream of air to one side and see how the ball is still hanging.

8 Balance the ball in the stream of air.

☆

9 Move the hair dryer and the ball toward the corner of a room. Look at how much higher the hanging ball moves.

What Happens

The ping-pong ball floats freely in the air. When you try to pull the ball out of the stream of air, you can feel a force pulling it back in. You can feel the ball turning the stream.

Why

- When the ball is hanging in the stream of air, the air flowing up hits the bottom of the ball.
- It slows and makes an area of higher pressure.
- The high pressure area of air under the ball holds the ball up against the pull of gravity.
- When you pull the ball a little bit out of the stream, the air flows around the curve of the ball that is nearest the center of the stream of air.
- Air rushes in an arc around the top of the ball. It then moves out above the ball.
- This outward flowing air puts out an inward force on the ball.

Fun Fact

The downward flow of air under a helicopter puts an upward force on the blades. The blades create lift by deflecting air downward.

I don't really care about the upward forces on the blades... or them creating lift... ...as long as they keep going around and around and around...

Mini Quiz
Why does air flowing over a surface in an arc put less pressure on that surface?

Mini Answer ✓
Think of a rider on a roller coaster going over the top of a hill at high speed. The force that the rider puts on the seat gets less as the rider goes over the top of the hill. In the same way, the air that arcs around the side of the ball puts less force on the ball.

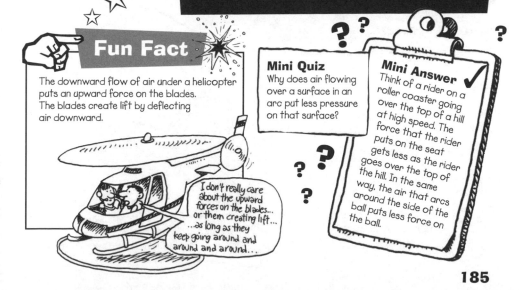

Smog Alert

(91)

Just goes to show... RAT made smog is just as bad as MAN made smog... now which way is out of the lab?

Rat's Rating

Smog is a mix of
natural fog – tiny
droplets of water in the
air and carbon dioxide
smoke from pollution.
It forms a thick, dirty,
smelly atmosphere.
Let's make some!

You will need:
glass jar, water, aluminum foil,
ice cubes, paper, ruler, scissors,
matches, ADULT SUPERVISION

What to do in this air experiment

1 Cut a strip of paper about 10 in. x 1/2 in. (25 cm x 1.25 cm).

2 Fold the length of the strip in half and twist the paper.

3 Make a "lid" for the glass jar by shaping a piece of aluminum foil over the open end of the jar. Take away the foil and put it aside.

4 Put some water in the jar. Swirl it around so the inside walls of the jar are wet.

5 Pour out the water.

6 Place 3 ice cubes on top of the foil lid to make it cold.

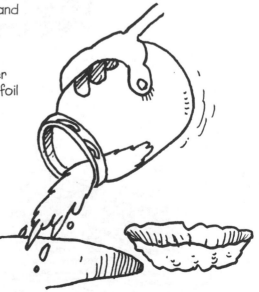

7 Ask an adult to light the strip of paper. Drop it and the match into the damp jar.

8 Quickly put the foil lid on the jar and seal it tightly. Keep the ice cubes on top of the foil, in the middle. What do you see in the jar?

What Happens
You have made smog!

Why
- When you put the lighted paper in the jar, you made some of the water moisture inside the jar evaporate into water vapor.
- The ice made a small amount of the water vapor condense. It turned into droplets of water in the jar. This appears as a mist in the jar.
- Warm damp air meets cold air. The cold air makes the moisture in the warm air condense into tiny droplets that are held in the air. If there is no wind, fog forms.

Fun Fact
The city of Los Angeles is very smoggy. At oxygen bars, you can buy pure oxygen. Twenty dollars gets you 20 minutes of plain or fruit-scented oxygen.

Mini Quiz
Can smog hurt you?

Mini Answer ✓
Smog is harmful to humans, animals, and plants. The most harmful parts of smog are ground-level ozone and fine airborne particles. The fog that shrouded London for 5 days in 1952 caused 4,000 deaths. Road, rail, and air transportation stopped. A show at the Sadler's Wells Theatre had to stop because the fog inside made it impossible to see.

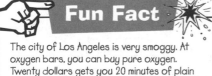

Hey buddy...! Give us $100 worth of the 'Lemon-Lime-Tangerine Dream Oxygen Mix'... Better make it snappy ...I'm about to pass out!

THE OXYGEN BAR LOS ANGELES

An Enlightening Experience

Where are You?

Rat's Rating

Boy! A pretty convincing fancy dress costume! LOOK! NO REFLECTION!

Can your reflection be here one moment, then gone the next?

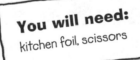

You will need:
kitchen foil, scissors

What to do in this light experiment

1 Use the scissors to cut a 10 in. (25 cm) length of kitchen foil from the roll. The foil must be smooth. Don't just tear it because it will go as wrinkly as a rat's tail!

2 Look at your reflection on the shiny side of the foil. It won't be perfect, but you'll see yourself quite clearly.

3 Scrunch the foil into a loose ball. Don't press it together tightly because you'll have to flatten it out again.

4 Flatten out the ball of foil

5 Look at your reflection. What do you see?

What Happens

Your reflection is gone!

AAHHR...I've vanished.!!

Why

- Light rays reflect from a surface in straight lines.
- When a surface is smooth, the rays are reflected back at you.
- When you make the smooth foil surface all scrunchy, the reflected light bounces off it in all directions.
- Because these reflected rays are going off at different angles, your image does not form in the way it did before.

Fun Fact

A rainbow is broken into bands of light. The reflection and refraction of the sun's rays in drops of rain make the rainbow. Reflection is simply the return of light waves from the surface of the raindrop. Light that looks white is really a mix of red, orange, yellow, green, blue, and violet light.

Unfortunately the rain stopped...and the rainbow disappeared before the guy looking for the pot of gold could find the end of the rainbow...

Mini Quiz
How can a big shiny spoon turn you upside down?

Mini Answer ✓
Hold a spoon up so you can see yourself in the scoop. Your reflection is upside down! When light is reflected from a curved surface, the rays leave the surface at different angles. Your reflected image is upside down because of the angle of the reflected rays of light.

93 Sunrise Sunset

Rat's Rating

When the Sun is up high...the light is white. In the afternoon... it's yellowy orange...

At night... without a flashlight .. It's BLACK !

Why does the sky change color at sunrise and sunset?

You will need:
clear drinking glass, water, whole milk, measuring cup, teaspoon, flashlight

What to do in this light experiment

1. Half fill a clear drinking glass with water.

2. Shine your flashlight through the glass from directly above. What color do you see?

3 Pour 1/2 cup of milk into the glass. Mix well.

★ ☆

4 Take the glass into a dark room. Shine a flashlight from the side. What do you see?

☆

What Happens

When the light is directly above the water, it looks white. This is like the sun when it's high in the sky. When the light shines on the milk, it looks yellow, orange, or red.

Why

- The earth is wrapped in a blanket of invisible gases. This is called the *atmosphere*.
- The atmosphere has billions of particles that are too small to see.
- When sunlight hits these particles, the light bounces off of them and scatters.
- When the sun is low in the sky in the morning and evening, its rays must travel through a thicker layer of atmosphere than at other times of the day.
- Orange and red light scatters the least. So you see these colors during sunrise and sunset.
- The particles of milk in the glass of water are like the atmosphere. They scatter some of the colors in the light from the flashlight.

Fun Fact

If there were no atmosphere, the sky would look black, like the lunar sky in *Apollo* pictures taken from the moon.

Come on...what's keeping you? We want to get home!

I'm waiting for a blue sky for the photo.

Mini Quiz
Why isn't the sky on Mars blue like the sky on Earth?

Mini Answer ✓
The Martian sky is a red color. This is because the air has dust in it. The dust particles have a mineral that soaks up sunlight at the blue end of the spectrum. The red wavelengths are left behind to color the sky. The atmospheric dust gives Mars its red color also.

94 To CD or Not CD

Rat's Rating

HICKORY DICKORY DOCK
THE RAT RAN UP
THE CLOCK...

RAT MUSIC

CD

Compact discs hold music, data, or computer software. But can you see light on them?

You will need:
a compact disc (also known as a CD), a sunny day (or a bright flashlight and a room that you can make dark), piece of white paper

What to do in this light experiment

1 Take the compact disc out of its case. Look at the side with no printing. What do you see?

2 You'll see bands of shimmering color. Tilt the CD back and forth and the colors will shift and change.

3 Hold the CD in the sunshine. Or, turn out the lights and shine your flashlight on the CD.

4 Hold your piece of white paper so that the light reflecting off the CD shines onto the paper.

5 What do you see now?

What Happens

You see rainbow colors on your paper. Tilt the CD and see how that changes the reflections. Change the distance from the CD to the paper. What happens to the colors?

Why

- Your CD is made of aluminum coated with plastic. The colors that you see on the CD are made by white light reflecting from ridges in the metal.
- The CD separates white light into all the colors that make it up.
- The colors you see reflecting from a CD are *interference* colors.
- When light waves reflect off the ridges on your CD, they overlap and interfere with each other.
- Sometimes the waves add together and make some colors brighter. They can also cancel out each other and take colors away.

Fun Fact

If you squint at a distant bright light at night, you'll see starburst patterns around the light. Look closely and you'll see colors in the patterns. These patterns are made when light bends around your eyelashes and specks in the lens of your eye. Tilt your head to one side while watching the pattern. See how the pattern moves with you.

What do you mean you spent 4 hours in the dark with your head tilted looking at distant lights?

I did it in the name of science!

Mini Quiz ❓
What color light is not a color?

Mini Answer ✓
White is not a color! It takes three colors of light to make up white light. These are called primary colors. There are many different sets of primary colors, but the most common for light are red, green, and blue. When red, green, and blue light are mixed in the proper strengths you get white light.

95 # Mirror Mirror

Rat's Rating

Ahhrr...beautiful! I've got a comb... and a MIRROR... now all I need is a flashlight for this next experiment...

Oh thanks!

When you look in a mirror, you see your reflection. But how do mirrors reflect light?

You will need:
comb, flashlight, piece of heavy paper, black sheet of paper, hand mirror, masking tape

What to do in this light experiment

1 Cut a hole in a piece of heavy paper about 1 in. (2.5 cm) in diameter.

2 Tape a comb across the hole.

3 Lay a black sheet of paper on the table, or use a dark surface.

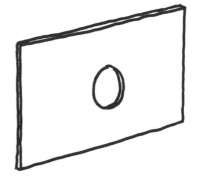

4 Go into a dark room. Place the card with the hole in front of the flashlight so that the narrow beams of light come from the teeth of the comb.

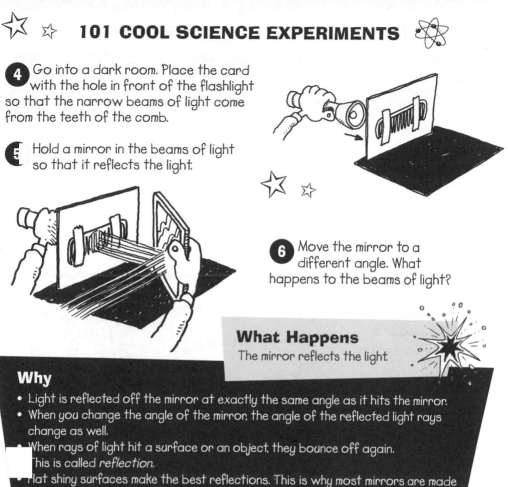

5 Hold a mirror in the beams of light so that it reflects the light.

6 Move the mirror to a different angle. What happens to the beams of light?

What Happens
The mirror reflects the light.

Why
- Light is reflected off the mirror at exactly the same angle as it hits the mirror.
- When you change the angle of the mirror, the angle of the reflected light rays change as well.
- When rays of light hit a surface or an object, they bounce off again. This is called *reflection*.
- Flat shiny surfaces make the best reflections. This is why most mirrors are made of flat sheets of highly polished glass with shiny silver coating behind them.

Fun Fact
You can write a secret message to friends using mirror code. Put a piece of paper in front of a mirror. Look in the mirror and carefully write your message on the paper. When you look at the paper, you'll see your message back to front in mirror code. Friends will be able to work out the message by looking in their own mirror.

O.K.! You look like a million dollars! PLEASE! I need the mirror now! I've got a very important MIRROR MESSAGE to decode!

Mini Quiz
If you wave at yourself in a mirror with your left hand, which hand does your reflection use?

Mini Answer ✔
Your right hand. Mirrors reverse images so that the left side appears to be the right.

96 Bent Light

Rat's Rating

An experiment on BENT LIGHT! Something tells me it's not _that_ sort of bent light!

Can light bend when it passes around an edge or through a slit? Find out.

You will need:
cotton handkerchief, lamp

Rat's Helpful Hint
Use a clean handkerchief.

What to do in this light experiment

1 Carefully take the lampshade off the lamp. Put it to one side.

2 Stand about 6 ft. (2 m) from the glowing bulb.

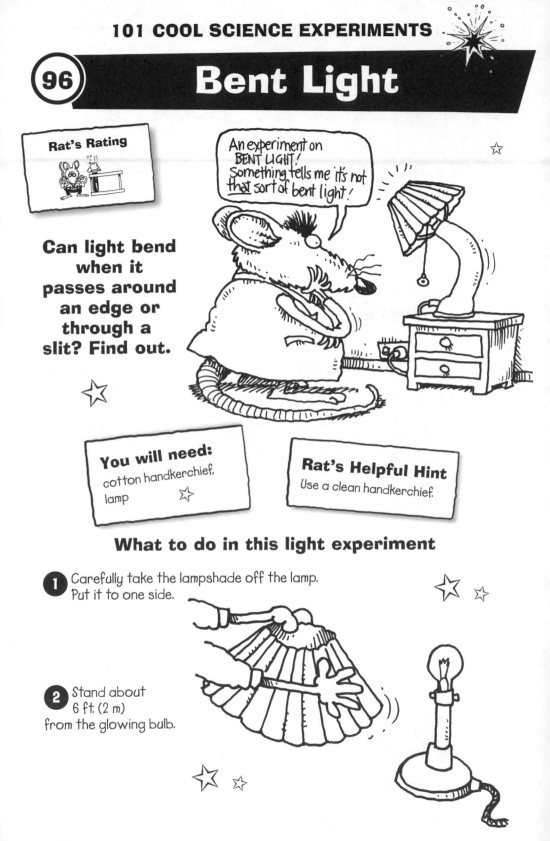

3 Look at the light through the stretched cloth. What do you see?

What Happens

A burst of light with dim bands of yellow and orange colors appears around the light.

Why

- The light bending or changing direction makes the starburst pattern.
- This bending is called *diffraction*.
- The dim bands between the light show that there is a wave joined with the light.
- The spaces between the woven threads in your handkerchief separate the light.
- The light waves spread and overlap. They come together in complicated ways to make the diffraction pattern that you see.
- Where the crest of one light wave overlaps with the crest of another wave, the two waves make a bigger wave. You then see a burst of light.
- Where the dip of one wave overlaps with the crest of another wave, the waves cancel one another out. You see a dark band.
- The holes in the weave of your handkerchief are large. You still see separate colors, but not as many as you would see through tiny holes.
- To make different patterns, try again with a feather or strands of hair.

Fun Fact

Drop a coin into the bottom of a drinking glass. Put your left hand on the side of the glass to block you seeing the coin. Pour water into the glass. The coin looks like it is floating on top of the water. Take away your hand. The coin now looks like it is floating and lying on the bottom. You are seeing the light rays coming from the coin. The water and glass make them bend so that you think you see the coins in two places at once.

If I can see twice as many coins... does that mean I have twice as much money?

Mini Quiz
Why does the handkerchief have different bands of color?

Mini Answer
The angle the light bends is in proportion to the wavelength of the light. Red light has a longer wavelength than blue light. It bends more than blue light does. This different amount of bending gives the bands their colored edges: blue on the inside, red on the outside.

97 Polar Bear Hair

What color is the skin of a polar bear?

You will need:
flashlight, clear drinking glass, empty aluminum cans, thermometers, white and black paper, scissors, water, measuring cup, notepaper, pencil

What to do in this light experiment

1 Shine your flashlight on a clear drinking glass. Does the glass let light pass through? A polar bear's hair lets light through too. The glass also reflects some light. Reflected light makes the polar bear's hair look white.

2 Some colors are better at soaking up the sun than others. Polar bear skin, under all of that hair, is the color that absorbs sunlight best. Now, is that color black or white?

3 Cover an aluminum can with white construction paper.

4 Cover another can with black.

5 Fill each can with 1 cup of water.

6 Place a thermometer in each cup.

7 Place both cans in full sun. Tilt them so that as much sunlight as possible hits the sides of the cans. Prop them in place with a book. Then tilt the thermometer so it gets as little direct sunlight as possible.

SUNLIGHT

BEARS OF THE NORTH

☆

8 Record the temperature of the water in each can. Record a new temperature every 5 minutes for 1/2 an hour. Which color is best at soaking up the warmth of the sun – white, or black? So what color is the skin of a polar bear?

What Happens
The water in the black can heats up faster than the water in the white can.

Why
- Anything dark, like black paper, will soak up more rays of the sun than anything white.
- The light energy is turned into heat.
- The white paper reflects the light before it can turn to heat.
- Polar bear hair and skin are adapted for Arctic climates. Each hair shaft is pigment-free and transparent with a hollow core.
- Polar bears look white because the hollow core scatters and reflects visible light, much like ice and snow.
- When photographed with film sensitive to ultraviolet light, polar bears look black.

Fun Fact
In 1979, three polar bears at the San Diego Zoo turned green. Scientists found out that algae was growing in the bears' hollow hair shafts. Although the algae didn't harm the bears, killing the algae with a salt solution made their fur white again.

Mini Quiz
Which gets hotter, land or water?

Mini Answer ✓
In sunlight, soil heats up faster. Land is darker than water and keeps the heat. In water, the heat goes deeper and spreads. Soil keeps the heat on the surface. If you dig into hot sand on the beach, the sand underneath is cool. Sunlight can't pass through it and the surface stays hot.

I know we all tried that GREEN fur last year.... But I reckon we should really lash out this year.

Yep! I see myself in PINK... HOT PINK!

I'm in Lavender... gold earrings ...black handbag and a large floral hat...

☆

Do You Know What's Watt?

Bright Spark

Rat's Rating

Who would have thought taking your clothes off in the dark would create an electrical storm!

Why does the air often crackle when you comb your hair or take off clothes? You'll be "ecstatic" when you find out.

You will need:
a time of year when the air is very dry, winter is a good time (this will not work when the air is humid), scissors, Styrofoam tray from your supermarket (ask at the meat or bakery counter for a clean tray), masking tape, aluminum pie tin

What to do in this electricity experiment

1 Cut a piece from one corner of the Styrofoam tray. You'll have a long bent piece that looks a bit like a hockey stick.

2 Cut a strip of masking tape. Tape the bent piece to the center of the pie tin to make a handle.

3 Rub the bottom of the Styrofoam tray on your hair. Rub it all over, very fast.

4 Put the tray upside down on a table.

5 Use the handle to pick up the pie tin. Hold it about 12 inches (30 cm) over the Styrofoam tray and drop it.

6 Very slowly, touch the tip of your finger to the pie tin. What happens? Don't touch the Styrofoam tray. If you do, nothing will happen!

What Happens

You make a bright spark! Use the handle to pick up the pie tin again. Touch the tin with the tip of your finger. You get another great spark. Drop the pie tin onto the Styrofoam tray again. Touch the pie tin. Another spark! Use the handle to pick up the pie tin. More sparks. If the pie tin stops giving you a spark, just rub the Styrofoam tray on your head again, and start over. Try this experiment in the dark. Can you see the tiny lightning bolts you make? What color are they?

Why

- When you rub Styrofoam on your hair, you pull electrons off your hair and they pile up on the Styrofoam.
- When you put the aluminum pie tin on the Styrofoam, the electrons on the Styrofoam pull on the electrons from the pie tin.
- Some of the electrons in metals are free electrons. This means they move inside the metal.
- Free electrons try to move as far away from the Styrofoam as they can.
- When you touch the pie tin, the free electrons leap to your hand. They spark!
- The pie tin now has fewer electrons. When you lift the pie tin away from the Styrofoam plate, you have a pie tin that attracts all nearby electrons.

Fun Fact

In 1752, Benjamin Franklin flew a kite and string in a thunderstorm. The electricity moved down the string. It made a small spark on the metal key near his hand. This showed that lightning was just a big spark of static electricity. He also invented the lightning rod to protect people, buildings, and ships from lightning. But, don't try this at home!

10 seconds after the now famous lightning bolt hit Benjamin's kite... ...a larger and more powerful bolt closed down his experiment...but drove him to invent the lightning rod

99 Be a Conductor

Rat's Rating

My faithful old rubber sandal. Are you a CONDUCTOR or an INSULATOR? That is the question!

Does electricity go through everything? Find out.

Rat's Helpful Hint

If you're barefooted, don't step on any electric wires. You might get a pair of shocks!

You will need:

spring type clothespin, 1 D-cell battery, aluminum foil or 2 plastic covered copper wires, flashlight bulb, masking tape, scissors, ruler, materials to test: safety pin, coins, cork, rubber band, leaf, water, paperclip, glass, plastic

What to do in this electricity experiment

1 If using copper wires skip to step number 5.

2 Cut the foil into a rectangle 24in. x 12 in. (60 cm x 30 cm).

3 Fold the foil in half along its length. Do this 5 times to make a thin strip 24 in. (60 cm) long.

FOLD FOIL TO MAKE ONE STRIP

4 Cut the foil strip in half to make two 24 in. (60 cm) strips.

5 Tape one end of both strips to the ends of the battery.

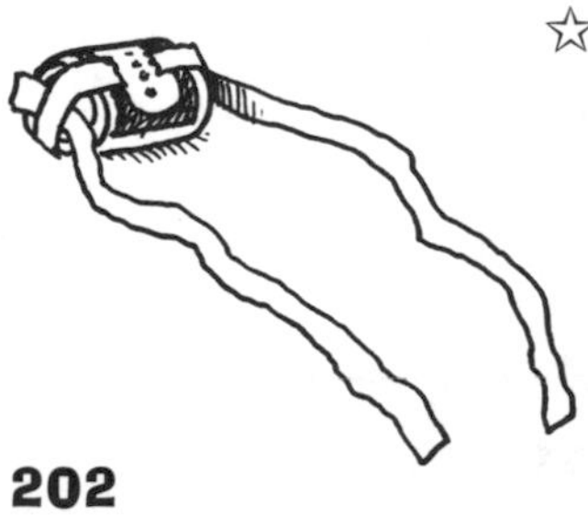

6 Wrap the other end of one strip around the base of the flashlight bulb. Fix the clothespin around the strip on the end of the lightbulb.

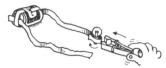

7 Test your materials to see if they conduct electricity. Touch the metal tip on the bottom of the flashlight bulb to one side of the material. At the same time, touch the free end of the metal strip to the opposite side of the same material.

TOUCH END OF BULB ON ITEMS TO TEST

What Happens

Some of your materials will let electricity flow through them and light the bulb. These materials are called *conductors*. Any living thing such as plants, animals, and trees are good conductors as well as wire, metal, and water. An *insulator* is a material that electricity doesn't easily flow through. Items such as plastic, rubber, and glass are good insulators.

Why

- An electric circuit is the path through which electrons move.
- A switch is a material that acts as a bridge for the electrons.
- When the circuit is closed by a switch, the electrons do not move freely.
- When it is open, the electrons move along the circuit.
- When you touch a good conductor and the tip of the bulb to the other side, you open a circuit.
- The electrons flow from the negative part of the battery through the foil conductor and into the bulb.
- The electrons go from the bulb through the foil and back into the positive end of the battery.
- As long as there is no break in the system, the electrons keep flowing and the bulb stays lit.

👉 **Fun Fact**

Electricity is measured in units of power called *watts*. It was named after James Watt, the inventor of the steam engine. One watt is a very small amount of power. It takes nearly 750 watts to equal 1 horsepower. A kilowatt equals 1,000 watts. The waste made by one chicken in its lifetime can supply enough electricity to run a 100 watt bulb for five hours!

So what are you calling your new unit to measure electricity sir?

WATT

I said what are you calling the new unit to measure electricity?

WATT

Forget it... we're getting nowhere here... I'll wait until I get my first power bill

Mini Quiz
Why must you never swim or play outdoors during a thunderstorm? ?

Mini Answer ✓
Lightning is a natural form of electricity. You are a good conductor of electricity. Being struck by lightning would kill you.

? ? ?

100 Glow Balloon

Rat's Rating

What happens when a balloon meets a fluorescent light?

You will need:
balloon, fluorescent light tube

GLOW BALLOONS... ...spooky!

What to do in this electricity experiment

1 Blow up the balloon. Seal it off.

2 Wash the outside of the fluorescent tube. Dry it well.

3 In a dark room, place one end of the tube against the floor.

4 Hold the tube upright. Quickly rub the balloon up and down the outside of it.

5 Hold the balloon near the tube.

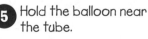

What Happens

The fluorescent tube starts to glow. The light moves with the movement of the balloon. Once the tube starts glowing, even the nearness of the balloon makes light.

Why

- A fluorescent light has tiny threads at each end. When the chemicals on the threads meet with an electrical current they make electricity.
- The electricity jumps from one end of the light to the other. It makes 120 flashes of light every second.
- Inside a fluorescent light is mercury vapor.
- The mercury vapor gives out ultraviolet light when an electric current passes through it.
- Your eyes don't see ultraviolet light. So, the inside of a fluorescent tube is coated with a phosphor. This coating changes the ultraviolet energy into light energy that you can see. We say the phosphor fluoresces.
- When you rub the balloon on the light, you make the same changes, but in a smaller way.
- Rubbing the balloon makes electrons build up on the balloon.
- This charges the mercury vapor inside the tube the same way electricity does.
- The charged mercury vapor gives off ultraviolet light. This makes the fluorescent chemicals inside the tube also give off light.

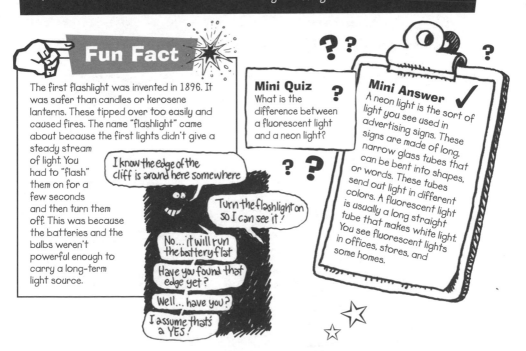

Fun Fact

The first flashlight was invented in 1896. It was safer than candles or kerosene lanterns. These tipped over too easily and caused fires. The name "flashlight" came about because the first lights didn't give a steady stream of light. You had to "flash" them on for a few seconds and then turn them off. This was because the batteries and the bulbs weren't powerful enough to carry a long-term light source.

Mini Quiz What is the difference between a fluorescent light and a neon light?

Mini Answer ✓ A neon light is the sort of light you see used in advertising signs. These are made of long, narrow glass tubes that can be bent into shapes, or words. These tubes send out light in different colors. A fluorescent light is usually a long straight tube that makes white light. You see fluorescent lights in offices, stores, and some homes.

(101) How Shocking!

Rat's Rating

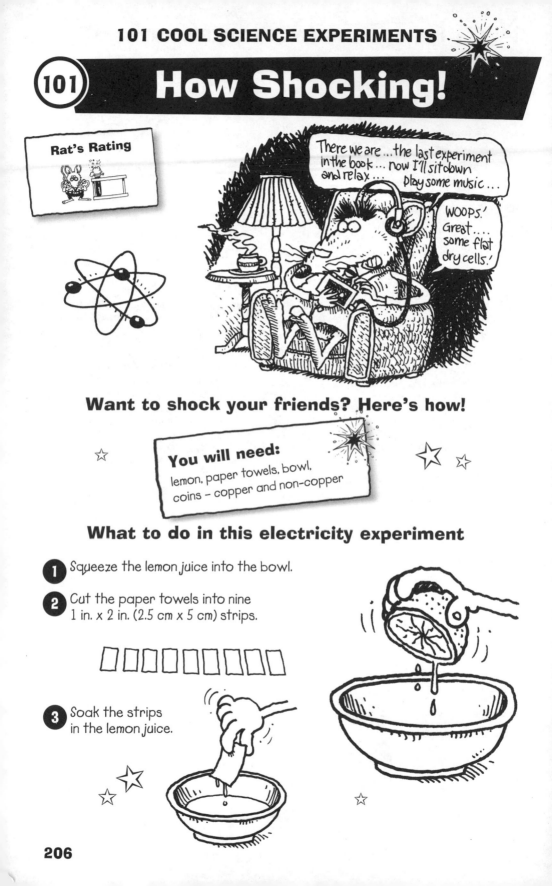

There we are ... the last experiment in the book ... now I'll sit down and relax ... play some music ...

WOOPS! Great .... some flat dry cells!

Want to shock your friends? Here's how!

You will need:
lemon, paper towels, bowl, coins – copper and non-copper

What to do in this electricity experiment

1 Squeeze the lemon juice into the bowl.

2 Cut the paper towels into nine 1 in. x 2 in. (2.5 cm x 5 cm) strips.

3 Soak the strips in the lemon juice.

4 Put down a copper coin. Lay a lemon soaked strip of paper on top.

5 Put a non-copper coin on top of the paper. Lay a lemon soaked strip of paper on top.

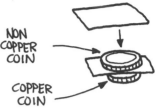

NON COPPER COIN

COPPER COIN

6 Repeat steps number 4 and 5 until you've made a tower of 10 coins – 5 copper and 5 non-copper.

7 Wet one fingertip of each hand.

8 Hold the coin tower between your fingers. What do you feel?

What Happens

You feel a small shock! This is because you've made a wet cell battery. Wet cells were used before batteries were invented.

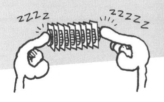

zzzz   zzzzz

Why

- The different metals in the two types of coins have different electrical strengths in their atoms.
- The lemon juice is a weak acid. It conducts an electric current between the two different coins.
- By having 5 sets of coins on top of each other, you have increased the electrical voltage of your battery. This is what you do when you put several batteries in a flashlight or radio.
- A battery is two or more dry cells. In each dry cell, 32 metals are separated by blotting paper soaked in a strong acid.

Fun Fact

The shock from an electric eel is about 650 volts. This is powerful enough to kill a horse and give a nasty shock to an elephant.

Out of all the waterholes in all of the world... I had to wade into the one with an ELECTRIC EEL!

NO SWIMMING ELECTRIC EELS

Mini Quiz

Why does a computer need a battery? Doesn't it get all of its power from the plug in the wall?

Mini Answer ✓

Most computers have a small battery that powers a chip called the *Real Time Clock* (RTC) chip. This quartz watch runs all the time, even when the computer is not on. The battery powers this clock. When the computer boots up, it asks the RTC to get the correct time and date.